10 STEPS

in *Writing* the RESEARCH PAPER

Peter T. Markman,
Professor Emeritus
Fullerton College
Fullerton, California
California State University, Long Beach
Long Beach, California

Alison L. Heney, Ph.D.,
Binghamton University
Binghamton, New York

Roberta H. Markman, Ph.D.,
Professor Emeritus
California State University, Long Beach
Long Beach, California

Marie L. Waddell,
Former Professor
University of Texas at El Paso
El Paso, Texas

BARRON'S

All inquiries should be addressed to:
Barron's Educational Series, Inc.
250 Wireless Boulevard
Hauppauge, NY 11788
www.barronseduc.com

ISBN: 978-0-7641-4598-8

Library of Congress Catalog Card No. 2011000493

Library of Congress Cataloging-in-Publication Data
Markman, Peter T.
    10 steps in writing the research paper / Peter T. Markman, Alison L.
    Heney, Roberta H. Markman ... [et al.] — 7th ed.
        p. cm.
    Includes bibliographical references and index.
    Previous ed.: 2001.
    ISBN 978-0-7641-4598-8
    1. English language–Rhetoric. 2. Research–Methodology. 3.
    Academic writing. I. Heney, Alison L. II. Markman, Roberta H. III. Title.
    IV. Title: Ten steps in writing the research paper.
    PE1478.M3 2011
    808'.042–dc22

                                                    2011000493

PRINTED IN THE UNITED STATES OF AMERICA
9 8 7 6 5 4 3 2 1

CONTENTS

PREFACE

We are delighted that the success of this manual in meeting the needs of both the high school and college student, as well as the graduate scholar now, on the forty-sixth anniversary of its first printing, warrants a seventh edition. Experienced research writers have profited from the manual's suggested techniques and the numerous models for correct form; inexperienced students have felt the security of being able to follow definite steps in order to write papers with the least wasted effort, the greatest accuracy in form, and the assurance that the finished papers would meet the most exacting standards of research. The methodology outlined here, the succinctness of its presentation, and the extensive coverage of its forms have received praise from both students and instructors throughout the country during the past forty-five years. We acknowledge here the work of the late Roberta Markman, the guiding force in the creation of the original book and the next five editions. Without her inspiration and her dedication, *10 Steps in Writing the Research Paper* would not exist. In its present form the book continues to reflect that inspiration and dedication. We also acknowledge the work of our late colleague Professor Emeritus Marie Waddell on the original edition of this manual. Her passing more than forty years ago was a great loss. We would also like to thank James L. Mitchell, MLS, Library Director of the Bainbridge-Guilford School District in New York, for his helpful guidance in our revising the materials on today's libraries.

Although this new edition retains the compact format for which the earlier five have been praised, the materials have been updated. It now includes full discussions of the use of the Internet for research, including the location and evaluation of electronic sources of research materials, reference guides to the Internet, and the proper parenthetical reference, footnote, and bibliographical forms to be used in documenting these materials in your research paper. There is also an updated list of style manuals and sources for basic reference. The documented paper has a profusion of accompanying footnotes and an extensive bibliography to illustrate every conceivable form and technique for the student. In addition, the outline for the paper is written to exemplify a comparative study with an interdisciplinary approach; it represents a new and important focus in education and a challenging area for further research. The sample paper itself is designed to develop only the thesis for the outline, but no problem of documentation is ignored.

We have each had the marvelous experience of sending our students off with this book as their only "instructor" and of receiving creative and accurately documented research in return. We therefore feel confident that this edition will do an even better job of instructing and of making the process of writing the research paper a process of ten easy steps.

HUNTINGTON HARBOUR, CALIFORNIA   *Peter Tollin Markman*
DECEMBER 1, 2010   *Alison Lynn Heney*

INTRODUCTION TO RESEARCH

Research is the disciplined process of investigating and seeking facts that will lead one to discover what one feels is the truth about something. In the beginning of the process of research, this "truth" is perhaps better seen as one's opinion, and the purpose of doing research then becomes finding the information to prove that this opinion should be considered true. This idea or opinion, stated as one's thesis,* is a result of the facts one discovers, and it must be proved conclusively to the reader by the facts selected. The thesis should not be a statement of preconceived opinion or prejudice, nor should the paper be merely a stringing together of related quotations and a collection of footnotes.

The research paper, a formal presentation of these discovered facts, provides the evidence one needs to defend the opinion expressed as the thesis. Consequently, one must state how and where these facts were found. If they were discovered from what other people have said or written, the student must tell who said them and where they were said so that the reader could find them also; if they were discovered by direct observation, the student must describe this experience so that the reader could repeat it and observe the same phenomena or facts. The opinion, which is the thesis, the analysis of the material on which it is based, and the conclusions one draws from that material are the most important parts of the final paper. These are subjectively presented while the facts, which provide the supporting points, are objectively presented and carefully documented.

During the process of research, the student learns to select, evaluate, and analyze facts; to discipline habits of thought and work; and, most important, to think—to create a new angle of vision. In this sense only, the research paper is original; but it is important enough in itself to justify the work involved in its creation.

Because nothing else so clearly reveals the true quality and merit of the writer's mind, the research paper becomes a valid criterion for judging the disciplined work habits and the intellectual maturity of the student.

---

*See Research Terms Defined, pp. 121 to 124.

THE TEN STEPS IN RESEARCH

There is always more than one way of accomplishing any task, and doing research is no exception. After much trial and error, the experienced researcher usually arrives at some system that has proved itself to be the best for him or her. However the individual systems may vary, there are ten basic steps that provide a logical method for research. They result in an ease of procedure for the researcher, the ultimate economy of time and effort, the assurance that comes from following a time-tested procedure, accuracy in the result, and the most universal acceptance by examining scholars. As you proceed, you may think that you can eliminate a step or two in the process, only to find later that you have created some extra ones to make up for the detour. So watch your step!

Step 1 FIND A SUBJECT.

Step 2 READ A GENERAL ARTICLE.

Step 3 FORMULATE A TEMPORARY THESIS AND A TEMPORARY OUTLINE.

Step 4 PREPARE THE PRELIMINARY BIBLIOGRAPHY.

Step 5 TAKE NOTES FROM RELEVANT SOURCES.

Step 6 LABEL NOTECARDS AND REVISE THE WORKING OUTLINE.

Step 7 WRITE THE FIRST DRAFT.

Step 8 REVISE THE TEXT; WRITE AN INTRODUCTION AND A CONCLUSION.

Step 9 COMPLETE AND CHECK PARENTHETICAL REFERENCES ON THE DRAFT.

Step 10 PUT THE PAPER IN FINAL FORM.

STEP

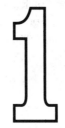

FIND A SUBJECT

Finding a topic that will interest you, one that is worth your time to investigate and one for which you will have the necessary time and materials, is an extremely important step in writing the research paper. You need not be familiar with a subject before doing research on it, but you should have some interest in the general area it involves because you will be working with that subject for a long period of time.

When the general subject is not assigned by your instructor, you can usually find one by examining your own interests, your background, or the other courses you are studying. There are other considerations that will limit the possibilities from which you may choose.

Your choice of a suitable subject for investigation will often be determined by whether or not you are interested in reading or investigating—and consequently analyzing—the original material directly and therefore working with primary sources* or whether you are interested in investigating what others have said about your subject and therefore working with secondary sources. The usual college assignment involves the latter. Your choice will be determined further when you eliminate unsuitable subjects. Some subjects are not worth investigating; they are either too trivial, merely factual, or obviously routine. Others are often too new or current for conclusive study; a research paper must be factual, not conjectural, and must therefore be based on a variety of dependable sources. The availability of resource

---

*See Research Terms Defined, pp. 121 to 124.

materials will vary somewhat with time and locale, so you must know your area and your library. And finally, some subjects have never been suitable for research: a biography summarized from secondary sources, the entire history of anything, or any subject that you will investigate with a closed mind.

STEP

READ A GENERAL ARTICLE

After you have decided on a subject, the next step is to read a general, authoritative article (such as one in the *Encyclopaedia Britannica* or *Americana*), browse through a scholarly book concerned with the general subject, or search the Internet so that you can see what the possibilities and ramifications of the subject are. You will, in this first investigation, find out whether a subject is too broad to use without strict limitation or too narrow to consider at all. You will also orient yourself and become familiar with the general area in which you will be working. This reading will not only suggest ideas about how you should begin to limit your chosen, general subject but will also suggest a number of possible theses inherent in it.

Sometimes a single sentence or phrase in this article will gain your attention and suggest a question you will want to investigate. In fact, if your chosen subject is at all interesting to you, it would be almost impossible to read any general article without finding phrases or sentences that will challenge you to investigate further some aspect of that subject. Look for ideas that prompt you to ask why or how they are true or in what specific way they may be true. These ideas will provide a basis upon which you will formulate a temporary thesis and a temporary outline (discussed in STEP 3).

If, for example, you are studying French and read a general article about France, you will find countless possibilities for research topics ranging from a comparative study of the French and American revolutions to the study of a particular influence (political, military, economic, religious) on the French character. If you are studying world literature and decide to write about Anton Chekhov (because you enjoyed seeing one of his plays), you might be alerted by any of the following statements: he contributed to the comic papers in Russia during the 1880s; he visited a convict island named Sakhalin and wrote a book about it that effected changes in the regime of that penal colony; his stories are developed along "calculated curves"; his masterpiece, *My Life*, is filled with symbols that give it an almost religious character. Such statements should arouse your curiosity, make you want to know more about some particular aspect of Chekhov's work, and send you searching for information that might substantiate any thesis you finally decide to develop. Certainly, such ideas would suggest many fascinating paths for you to explore.

Any time you browse through an encyclopedia, or a book, or an Internet site, you will find wonderful surprises and delightful reading that may prove to be "an arch wherethro' gleams that untravelled world" of knowledge and understanding that awaits all students. Some subject you once thought or heard about but never had a chance to pursue may challenge you to look into its various implications. Even a cursory reading of almost any general article will certainly prove that your problem will never be one of not finding some idea to research; your only problem will be deciding which of the myriad facets of knowledge on life you will choose to investigate and then reveal in your research project. No matter what thesis suggests itself as you read an encyclopedia article, book, or web page, your pursuit of it will enable you to take a giant step toward an increased perception, awareness, and enjoyment of the all-too-often hidden world around you.

STEP

FORMULATE A TEMPORARY THESIS AND A TEMPORARY OUTLINE

After you have found a general subject and have read a general article for background, you must next decide how you will work with the topic you have chosen. You might, for example, have selected several authors as the subject of your paper. You will have access to books and articles that deal with facts about their personal lives, their work, their environment, the influences on their lives and work, and the significance of their influence on others. Certainly, there would be no value in simply restating the facts and opinions as you have read them; you could not retell them all, and you would have no criterion for deciding how to select those that you would retell. Consequently, you will have to decide to concentrate on some point that your preliminary reading has suggested is an arguable truth about your topic and that further reading would probably substantiate and clarify. Just as the creative artist is led to make a statement of truth about some aspect of life by observing and selecting from the myriad details of life's experiences, so you, as a researcher, must be able to crystallize a statement of truth by observing and selecting significant details from the wealth of material you will find on your topic. This truth, stated in a simple sentence, provides you with a temporary thesis. It is a statement of your opinion, a conclusion that, from what you have read, you have reason to believe can be proven, but that you are scholar enough to discard or alter later if you uncover facts that prove it limited or invalid. A good thesis is never the statement of a preconceived notion or a personal prejudice that you could prove only by distorting or ignoring facts, nor is it the statement of any indisputable fact about which further investigation would reveal nothing. It must express an idea that is arguable or debatable or one that demands further explanation. Because it is an idea, it must be expressed as a full sentence, never just a phrase. "Mythology as art" is a subject, not a thesis. "A culture often expresses its mythology both visually and verbally" is an acceptable thesis. As a thesis, it requires further explanation and research because it is not self-explanatory.

If, for example, you wanted to do your research on some area of mythology, you might find in the course of your reading that you are surprised to learn that the Greeks portrayed even their most important gods and goddesses, such as Zeus and his wife Hera, as people like themselves who, although powerful and immortal, had many human frailties. The almighty Zeus, for example, was often guilty of thievery and promiscuity, as well as trickery to hide his many infidelities from his wife. Your discovery would not, however, justify a thesis that states that most Greek myths are just stories that show how evil the major gods are. Such a thesis would be based on a preconceived notion showing the limitations of your own understanding of the complexity of the subject. Neither would you consider a thesis statement saying that many early societies developed their own mythologies about the lives of the gods because this is an indisputable fact and there is very little to argue with or prove. However, because you might have realized from reading further that each culture differs dramatically in the way it thinks about the nature of its gods, you might consider an investigation of the similarities and differences in the ways that two, or possibly even three, different cultures look at their gods or how they conceptualize the relationship of mankind to the gods they have created.

Or perhaps as a result of reading in a general article that there are many similarities between African creation myths, which tell how the world and mankind came into being, and myths concerning death and the mystery surrounding death, you might be challenged to investigate the relationship between the creation and fertility myths and myths about death in the mythology of the Korumba people of Africa.

On the other hand, you might have been alerted by a statement in a general article that explains how a particular Mexican mask is used in a ritual that "acts out" the story of a myth about the Aztec god Quet-zalcoatl. You might decide to show how the details of the myth are translated into the specific actions of a ritual. Or you might be interested in finding out how and why certain rituals are practiced in some areas of Mexico and absent from others. In other words, you will choose one aspect of what you have read and investigate it to ascertain its validity.

Or after attending an exhibition of ancient Egyptian art and reading the catalog from it, you might realize how valuable it would be to know something about Egyptian mythology; you might even wonder whether there is a strong relationship between the art you saw at the museum and the Egyptian myths you find in your library. That question could challenge you to formulate a thesis that involves a study of the relationship of art and mythology in ancient Egypt or in another early culture that you would like to investigate. However, you would see very quickly that, because of the innumerable perspectives from which art and mythology can be compared, there are too many possibilities for development in one paper. Therefore, you might scan general articles covering various aspects of Egyptian mythology as well as of Egyptian art to find out whether there is some concept common to both that could form the basis of a comparative study of the two. You might find, for example, that Egyptian creation myths are the subjects of much of the art that attempts to express visually the mythology of "the beginning." A comparative study of the two modes of expression would now give you a basis upon which to narrow and reformulate your temporary thesis.

Although the thesis that you develop now is necessarily a temporary one because you have not accumulated all the available facts yet, it does provide you with an angle of vision from which you can continue your research. You now know how you are going to focus on your subject, and you are ready to formulate a temporary outline. As you search in your reading and note-taking for the answers to the challenging question suggested by your thesis, you will, of course, reevaluate your facts and modify your first opinion until you are closer to the ultimate truth, the discovery of which is always the purpose of your research.

It is important to limit your temporary thesis as soon as possible so that, within the limits of the time in which you have to work and the projected or assigned length of the finished paper, the truth of that thesis statement can be investigated thoroughly. No factor is more often responsible for a poor research paper than is the failure to limit a thesis. It is obvious that the less area you try to cover, the more depth you can explore and the more valuable your finished paper will be. As you do your research, you will probably keep narrowing your thesis and limiting the scope of your research to express an idea that can be thoroughly and realistically handled within the space limitation of your paper.

One way to help you limit your thesis is to write a very short, preliminary temporary outline listing in sentence form the main ideas that you hope to develop in order to prove your thesis. Then look to see if any one of those points might serve as the thesis itself. Continue to go through that process until you feel you have limited your thesis as much as possible. Although this thesis is necessarily a temporary one because you have not accumulated all the available facts yet, it does provide you with an angle of vision from which you can continue your research. You now know how you are going to focus on your subject and how you are going to select the material for your research. You are ready now to formulate a more complete temporary outline.

TEMPORARY OUTLINE

The particular angle of vision of your limited thesis will automatically suggest and determine the temporary outline you need to work with. If you formulate a thesis stating that humanity's attempt to understand the basic phenomena of life is expressed symbolically both verbally in mythology and visually in art, you would be compelled to investigate the truth of that statement. You would need to (1) find out how and to what extent mythology and art are symbolically expressed, (2) discover what basic phenomena of life are expressed both visually and verbally, and (3) consider how and to what extent the visual and verbal expression are comparable in expressing the attitudes and beliefs of their respective cultures. At this point you still may not be certain that you can find a sufficient basis for comparison, but it is obvious from the outset that these three basic concerns, which constitute the points of your temporary outline, must be investigated before you can conclusively state your thesis as truth. Similarly, a logical analysis of any thesis that you choose to work with will suggest the points for your temporary outline. It is important that you state them as sentences because only a sentence can state a complete idea. Then when you put them into the temporary outline, you will know exactly the point that you are going to make. They outline the path along which you and your reader must travel before the statement you first wrote as a temporary thesis can be stated as a valid conclusion and become your final thesis. A topic outline made up of words or phrases rather than statements in sentence form is too ambiguous to accomplish this task.

With the formulation of your thesis as a temporary objective and with an outline statement of the points by which you can logically reach it, you have the necessary criteria by which, with a minimum of wasted effort, to select books for your bibliography (STEP 4) and to choose information for your notecards (STEP 5).

In setting up your temporary outline you are actually using a deductive process. You have temporarily accepted a general statement or premise, and you are going to investigate your sources to see whether or not that premise can be substantially supported by facts. Because a generality would be too superficial to work with unless it is supported by specific and valid evidence, it is extremely important that you use the most authoritative sources available from which to find your information. You must be wary of unsigned editorial columns, magazine articles, or websites that are not carefully documented. For this reason, also, you must consult many different sources representing a wide range of thinking in order to make your paper valuable as research. However, in spite of the fact that your temporary outline is the result of a deductive process, your final thesis and outline must be inductively developed. That is, you must eventually analyze your material or the facts accumulated and change your temporary thesis so that it ultimately states an accurate result or conclusion of the material you have observed and presented. The temporary thesis, then, is the statement of a hunch or of an educated guess; the final thesis is the result of research and is a statement of what you now believe to be true. You see it as the only conclusion to which one could come from the material that you have selected and presented. And your outline shows the means by which you arrived at your thesis so that your reader can follow the process step by step with you. See STEP 6 for further help in writing your outline.

STEP

PREPARE THE PRELIMINARY BIBLIOGRAPHY

WHY A PRELIMINARY BIBLIOGRAPHY IS NECESSARY

There are several reasons why, before you begin to do your research, it is important to prepare a preliminary bibliography even though it will include books you will never see or use.

1. You must be sure that adequate information on the subject is available to you and that your thesis is not hackneyed.

2. You must allow time to order any pertinent published materials that you may need to obtain through the interlibrary loan service. There is often a nominal charge for postage, and you should be prepared to wait at least a week.

3. You need to become familiar with the type of research that has been done on your topic.

4. From seeing a variety of titles, you will learn how your chosen thesis might be further limited or broadened.

5. You will be given clues about titles, subjects, and authors relating to your particular subject; for example, in looking up *Mythology*, you will find a section on *Creation Myths* which would lead you to *Types of Creation Myths* or *Origins of Creation Myths* as well as *Theories of Creation Myths* and thence to the specific names of mythologists who have much to say about creation myths, such as Sir James Frazer or Joseph Campbell.

6. As you prepare your bibliography and later as you browse through the material, it is urgent that you evaluate and critically examine your sources. Certainly not everything in print or available through the Internet is valuable. By considering some important questions you will be able to evaluate your sources with some confidence:

   a. Does the author document sources in footnotes at the bottom of the page or endnotes at the end of a chapter or book or Internet site? It is important to know where the information that you are reading came from. Does the author include a bibliography? This is an indication of the author's awareness of other research that has been done in the field.

   b. What is the date of the publication you are using and of the sources the author is using? If your topic requires current information, outdated material will be of no use, and if further research has been done even on something that is not current, what you say will mean very little.

   c. Is the author an authority in the field? Often the book jacket or information at the beginning or end of an article or Internet site gives the author's credentials. You might want to check in such works as the *Dictionary of American Scholars* or *American Men and Women of Science* to find out something about the author's background.

   d. Have you seen references to the author in the bibliographies of other works dealing with the same subject? Usually experts in a particular field are referred to frequently in other works.

   e. Who has published or sponsored the material? A university press usually publishes scholarly, well-researched material and some of the best known publishers are usually reliable. However, a vanity press or a popular magazine would normally not be a valuable source, whereas periodicals that cater to specialists would be.

f. Is this Internet site reliable and authoritative? The caution with which you approach research materials applies even more to Internet sites than to print material. The existence of a link to a site on Google is absolutely not a guarantee of that site's reliability. Often the titles of these sites are misleading, indicating for example, that they are "the official" site of this or that organization when, in fact, they are no such thing. An Internet site created by an individual may be called anything that individual wishes to call it and may contain anything he or she wishes to put there. You must be extremely careful in using these sites, but fortunately there are several criteria that can help you to evaluate them in addition to those previously listed. The Internet address is the first indicator. Sites in the *.edu* and *.gov* domains are likely to be trustworthy since they are affiliated with educational and governmental institutions, just as books and journals published by university presses and governmental agencies are likely to be authoritative. Be particularly wary of free sites available to individuals in the *.com* domain. Second, look at the sites from which the site you are evaluating may be reached. If an authoritative site includes a link to this site, that is a good indication that it has been evaluated positively by an authority in that field. Third, make use of the available means of evaluating sites. The Internet Public Library <*http:/www.ipl.org*>, for example, has links to sites it has evaluated. While these pointers can help you to evaluate a site, probably the best advice is to be cautious and use the knowledge you have accumulated. If a particular site has information or ideas you find nowhere else, be suspicious

g. Is the book, article, or website giving you information that is the result of the author's research, or is it merely a compilation of material from books and articles, such as an encyclopedia (the *Encyclopaedia Britannica*, for example, or an online encyclopedia such as Wikipedia)? Such sources are basically research papers themselves, so you should try to find original sources rather than relying on these secondary ones. Wikipedia, available online only, should be used with special caution since its millions of articles are contributed by great numbers of volunteers. Although these articles are screened by other volunteers, the potential for the spread of misinformation is relatively high. Thus Wikipedia, while useful for some things, cannot be considered authoritative.

WHERE TO FIND A PRELIMINARY BIBLIOGRAPHY

There are many places where you will find a listing of materials that you can include in your preliminary bibliography, but the two primary sources are your library and your computer. Of course, your bibliography will change considerably before it becomes final because many of the titles you find in your preliminary search will not be available, some will not be useful, and you will add new sources constantly as you come across them in your reading. Do not look in only one place for your sources; use the library* as well as the Internet. Try to investigate all of the resources available to you.

SEARCHING FOR MATERIALS IN THE LIBRARY

Most libraries provide two types of computer searches. The first enables you to search among all the holdings that exist in the library itself. This is the computerized version of the old card catalog and periodical indexes. Second, you may access online databases including bibliographies or indexes, or print out full texts.

1. Searching for Materials Housed in the Library

You may do a computer search for materials in the library on the library's computers, or if you wish, you can probably log on to your library's catalog from your own personal computer. Ask the librarian if you have any concerns about how to use the library's computers or how to access the material using your own computer.

---

*See also Library Classification Systems, pp. 150 to 151. See also Reference Materials and Style Manuals, pp. 152 to 159.

EXAMPLE OF AN ENTRY IN THE ONLINE CATALOG (ALSO CALLED OPAC)

```
BL311          C263          1986
Campbell, Joseph, 1904–1987

The inner reaches of outer space: metaphor as myth
and as religion.

PUB INFO:   Joseph Campbell.
            New York: A. van derMarck Editions,
            c1986.
DESCRIPT:   155 p.: ill. (some col.); 25 cm.
NOTE 1:     Includes bibliographical references and
            index.
SUBJECT 1:  Mythology.
SUBJECT 2:  Religion.
SUBJECT 3:  Metaphor—Religious aspects.
ISBN:       0912383097
LCCN:       84-40776
OCLC NO:    #13008516
```

NOTE: Computer systems vary in different libraries, so the format may be different in your library, but the information will be similar.

The second type of computer search accessing online databases can be done for free through your library. Lexis/Nexis, for example, allows you access to more than one hundred terabytes of content. Others such as Proquest and InfoTrac are also very large. They all catalog a wide range of subjects, such as government, humanities, physical science, business, education, and health. This material can usually be located according to author or subject. Such a search will produce a list (or the entire article) of references, mainly to journal and newspaper articles, on the topic being researched. Since there is a wide variety of databases that will make all kinds of information available to facilitate your search, be sure to ask the librarian for a list of available databases and what they contain.

There are two types of databases: bibliographic and full text. The former consists of a list of bibliographic references to articles and often includes a short abstract of particular ones. The full text databases include both the references and the full text of the article.

An effective and economical search depends on your advance preparation for it:

a. The first step is to set up a "search statement" such as: "Mesoamerican rituals involve images, symbols, myths."

b. From this statement identify the main concepts or keywords that will be used in the search: "images," "symbols," "myths," "rituals," "Mesoamerica."

c. Look over the areas on the particular databases that are available to you and find those that are appropriate for your particular search.

d. Then you will use a printed database thesaurus, which has more keywords for your database, to help you describe your research needs or make up your own keywords to add to the previous ones, such as: "costumes," "mythology," "cosmology," "spirituality," "religion," "gods," "Mexico."

e. Decide how to limit or expand these concepts to get closer to what you are looking for, such as "Mexican mythology," "Mexican rituals" in a particular century or place, and so on.

You are now ready to use the computer and enter your research terms. You may simply read the material on the screen, print the results, download the results onto a disc or jump drive, or do all of these.

The screen will let you know how many articles the keywords you have entered will generate. If you find too many entries that are not relevant, you can limit your keywords and ask for articles that have only "Mexican and mythology" involved or "symbols and rituals in Mexico." If you find that there will be too few entries, you can expand the possibilities by asking for "masks or rituals or mythology in Mexico." Obviously the more terms you plug in, the narrower the search will be. For example, the term "mythology" will yield much more material than "Mesoamerican mythology," and if you specify a particular kind of myth, such as "Mesoamerican creation myths," there will be even less material.

An online search is an exciting research experience and will help to immerse you in your subject. Even the titles that appear will, in themselves, be valuable in giving you ideas for your paper and suggest ways to develop and qualify your own thesis, and you will be confident to know that others before you have successfully explored the same area that you have chosen to investigate.

2. Searching for Material on the Internet

On the Web you will find information gathered by universities, libraries, museums, medical providers, non-profit organizations, corporations and businesses, and many other groups and individuals.

Each of these collections of information is found at a website and each website has its own address, or URL, which looks like this:

---

http://www.columbia.edu/cu/cup/cgos/basic.html

*http://*indicates that this is a World Wide Web site.

www.columbia.edu is the main address and indicates that this is the web site of Columbia University; *.edu* is the name of the domain, or segment of the World Wide Web, where this site is located; *edu* indicates an educational institution. Other domain names are *.gov* indicating a governmental body; *.org* indicating an organization; and *.com* indicating a commercial enterprise. The domain of the site is an important indicator of its value and trustworthiness. While much valid and useful information can be found on *.org* and *.com* sites, they must generally be used with more caution than *.edu* and *.gov* web sites.

/cu/cup/cgos/basic are progressively smaller subdivisions of the large Columbia University web site; they mark the path to your information. This address, then, will take you directly to the part of the Columbia University site you want.

.html stands for Hypertext Markup language and indicates the format used in this web site.

Of course you will not know the address for all the sites that may prove useful in your research project. To locate them you will use a search engine that will search a portion of the Web for the information you specify. Although no single search engine searches the entire Web, Google has become the most widely used. In addition to its very large database, it has two features, Google Scholar and Google Books, that make it particularly useful for research since they are designed to lead the researcher to authoritative information. These features may currently be found by opening "About Google." In addition, of course, you may use other search engines in order to maximize your chances of finding useful sites. Although there are two different types of search engines—directories and what are more precisely called search engines—they can be used interchangeably for your purposes. Directories allow you to search by subject categories, and you must try to define your category as narrowly as possible in order to exclude large amounts of irrelevant material. (See discussion of such limiting on p. 20.) Search engines allow you to search by entering a key word or words. Again it is important to be as precise and limited as possible. The "advanced search" and "help" features of each search engine give you a number of useful pointers in limiting your search. If you want the search engine to find all of and only the exact wording you enter, you must generally enclose that wording in quotations.

Other search engines and directories that may prove useful in addition to Google include:

Altavista	*http://www.altavista.com*
Bing	*http://www.bing.com*
HotBot	*http://www.hotbot.com*
Lycos	*http://www.lycos.com*
WebCrawler	*http://www.webcrawler.com*
Yahoo!	*http://www.yahoo.com*

In addition to finding relevant sources through the use of search engines and directories, you will also locate relevant sites through links on the sites you have already found, much as you would find other useful books and articles through references in books and articles you have read. These links can lead you from site to site on the World Wide Web and make clear to you the appropriateness of the spider's web as a metaphor for this amazing network of information.

You may also find sources of information for your research paper through a number of specialized directories that are often called virtual libraries. These directories generally evaluate the quality of the sources they include and often provide useful annotation indicating the nature of the resource. The best known of these are:

Britannica   *http://www.britannica.com*
Infomine   *http://www.ucr.edu*
Internet Public Library   *http://www.ipl.org*
LibrarySpot   *http://www.libraryspot.com*
Project Muse   *http://muse.jhu.edu*
The Virtual Reference Desk *http://www.virtualref.com*

Since you must be very cautious in your use of Internet sources, such sites as these are particularly valuable because they carefully screen the sites they list. It is often very difficult for you to know on your own whether a given site contains trustworthy information placed there by an authoritative source. A recommendation by one of these virtual libraries is a form of insurance that your research paper will be supported by valid information.

Doing your own search for materials can be fun, especially if you enjoy working with computers and discovering their capabilities. Fortunately, the library is set up for students to work on their own, and there are librarians ready to help, should a problem arise. The computers generate very clear step-by-step instructions on the screen to help you with your search strategy and database selection. Check with a librarian if you are not getting the results you want in your own search. He or she will probably be aware of a broader range of databases that could be helpful. If you would like to have a librarian conduct the search for you, check to see how that can be arranged and whether there will be a fee.

HOW TO WRITE YOUR BIBLIOGRAPHY CARDS

The traditional way of recording the information you have gathered in putting together your preliminary bibliography was to enter the bibliographical information from each source on a 3 × 5-inch index card. That method would enable you to organize and reorganize your sources in different ways, such as separating those you have already read from those you have not, and arranging them alphabetically, topically, and chronologically.

Now, however, many researchers use a computer to record this information. There are, in fact, programs designed to facilitate using your computer for this purpose.

In our discussion here, we will outline the traditional procedure, but you may, of course, modify it to suit the technology you are using. However you do it, though, it must be done, since this bibliographical information will be vital in finding sources of material and in documenting your use of that material. In some cases you will only have your notes and not the original book or article when the time comes to write your footnotes and final bibliography, so accuracy in recording this information is vital.

In order to save time and effort, you should make up your cards with whatever information you have, leaving lines and spaces to be completed when you have the actual book or other source in your hands.

On the back of the bibliography card put the call number and/or the place where you found out about this source. Also put any other information to which you might want to refer later. You will also use the back of the card to annotate your bibliography when you have seen the book. See pp. 63 and 116.

As we have already discussed (see pp. 18 to 23), research materials are now found in two different media: print and electronic. The basic source for print media is, of course, the library, while electronic media is available to you through your personal computer. Within each of these two categories, there are two basic bibliographic forms:

Print Media:

1. There is a basic form for a source that is not part of a larger work (pp. 25 to 32).

2. There is a basic form for a source contained within a larger work (pp. 32 to 40).

Electronic Media:

1. There is a basic form for a source that is not part of a larger work (pp. 40 to 43).

2. There is a basic form for a source contained within a larger work (pp. 43 to 46).

While the models we have included for print media sources cover practically all of the bibliographic situations you will encounter, the situation is somewhat different for the models for electronic media sources. New types of sources and variations of old ones are still being created. In case you encounter a source that varies significantly from the models we have provided, you must modify the form that is closest to what you have found, keeping in mind that you always need to provide your readers with the basic information they will need to locate the document. In addition, we have not included as many models for electronic sources as we have for print sources since in the case of multiple authors, editors, and translators; and so on, you can easily use the print media model to modify the basic electronic media model.

These sample cards are based on the MLA format (see p. 49), but the information on them is necessary no matter which of the several possible forms you finally use. You will note that each card carries a notation indicating the medium of publication (for example, "print" or "Web") as that is required in the new MLA format. You should also note that in your final paper it is preferable to italicize—rather than underline—the titles of works so that, if you are using your computer to prepare these cards, you may italicize rather than underline these titles.

We begin each section with a card illustrating the basic form and then present a series of cards with models for various possibilities.

PRINT MEDIA

FORM FOR A SOURCE THAT IS NOT PART OF A LARGER WORK

(Note: You need not have used or read the entire work.)

```
Campbell, Joseph.
The Inner Reaches of Outer Space: Metaphor
  as Myth and as Religion.
New York: Alfred van der Marck Editions,
1986. Print.
```

1st line: author's name in inverted order
> (If there are two or more authors, use the following form in example 3, 4, or 5).

> end punctuation: period

2nd line: title of book

(Capitalize the first and last word and all other words except CAPs—short conjunctions, articles, and short prepositions; underline each word separately to indicate title as it appears on outside of book; underlining is a substitute for italics.)

end punctuation: period

3rd line: facts of publication and medium of publication

(Place of publication followed by colon and name of publisher.)

end punctuation: comma

NOTES: As place of publication, give only the city in which the publisher is located as indicated on the title page of the book. If more than one city is given, use only the first. You should write the name of the publisher exactly as it appears on the title page, abbreviating and capitalizing only those words that are abbreviated and/or capitalized. However "University Press" as part of a publisher's name (i.e., Ohio State University Press) may be abbreviated "UP" (i.e., Ohio State UP).

If the publisher is not given, write the abbreviation in brackets thus: [n.p.]

4th line: date of publication and medium of publication

(Whenever more than one date of publication or copyright is given, use the most recent one. If no date is given, write the abbreviation in brackets thus: [n.d.]). The date of publication is followed by a period and the medium of publication.

end punctuation: period

PRINT MEDIA

MODELS FOR A SOURCE THAT IS NOT PART OF A LARGER WORK

1. the basic form

```
Campbell, Joseph.
The Inner Reaches of Outer Space: Metaphor
   as Myth and as Religion.
New York: Alfred van der Marck Editions,
1986. Print.
```

2. no author

Máscaras Mexicanas: de la Colección
  del Ing. Victor José Moya.
México: Dirección de Museos del
  Instituto Nacional de Antropología
  e Historia,
1974. Print.

3. two authors

Markman, Roberta H., and Peter T. Markman.
The Flayed God: The Mesoamerican Mythological
  Tradition.
San Francisco: Harper San Francisco,
1992. Print.

4. three authors

Broda, Johanna, Davíd Carrasco, and Eduardo
  Matos Moctezuma.
The Great Temple of Tenochtitlan: Center and
  Periphery in the Aztec World.
Berkeley: U of California P,
1987. Print.

5. more than three authors

Lothrop, Samuel K., and others.
Essays in Pre-Columbian Art and Archaeology.
Cambridge, Massachusetts: Harvard UP,
1961. Print.

NOTE: The author line may be thus:
        Lothrop, Samuel K., et al.

6. corporate authorship

Instituto Guerrerense de la Cultura.
Calendario de Fiestas del Estado de Guerrero.
Chilpancingo, Guerrero, México: Instituto
  Guerrerense de la Cultura,
1987. Print.

7. an author and an editor

Campbell, Joseph.
The Power of Myth with Bill Moyers.
Ed. Betty Sue Flowers.
New York: Doubleday,
1988. Print.

8. an author and a translator

Eliade, Mircea.
Images and Symbols.
Trans. Philip Mairet.
Kansas City: Sheed Andrews
  and McMeel,
1961. Print.

9. an author, an editor, and a translator

Neruda, Pablo.
A New Decade (Poems: 1958-1967).
Ed. Ben Belitt.
Trans. Ben Belitt and Alastair Reid.
New York: Grove Press,
1969. Print.

10. an editor but no author

Apostolos-Cappadona, Diane, ed.
<u>Symbolism, the Sacred, and the Arts</u>.
New York: Crossroad,
1988. Print.

NOTE: This form would be used when referring to an anthology as a whole, rather than one of the works included in the anthology, as well as for any other book with an editor but no author.

11. a translator and an editor but no author

Sullivan, Thelma D., trans.
A <u>Scattering of Jades: Stories, Poems, and Prayers
  of the Aztecs</u>.
Ed. T. J. Knab.
New York: Simon and Schuster,
1994. Print.

NOTE: The translator precedes the editor on the title page of this book, and the bibliography card follows that order.

12. a compiler

Muser, Curt, comp.
<u>Facts and Artifacts of Ancient
  Middle America</u>.
New York: E. P. Dutton,
1978. Print.

13. one volume is a multivolume set when all volumes have the same title

Budge, E. A. Wallis.
<u>The Gods of the Egyptians or Studies
  in Egyptian Mythology</u>, 2 vols.
1904;
rpt. New York: Dover Publications,
1969, Vol. 2. Print.

NOTE: This is a modern reprint of a book originally published in 1904. See example 18.

14. one volume in a multivolume set when each volume has a separate title

```
Coe, Michael D., and Richard A. Diehl.
The People of the River.
Vol. 2 of In the Land of the Olmec. 2 vols.
Austin: U of Texas P,
1980. Print.
```

15. a book in a series edited by one other than the author

```
Maclagen, David.
Creation Myths: Man's Introduction to
  the World.
In the Art and Imagination series.
Ed. Jill Purce.
London: Thames and Hudson,
1977. Print.
```

NOTE: If the volumes were numbered, the third line would be thus: Vol. 2 of Art and Imagination, as in example 14.

16. a book with a subtitle or secondary title

```
Hopper, Vincent F., ed. and trans.
Chaucer's Canterbury Tales: An Interlinear
  Translation.
Woodbury: Barron's,
1970. Print.
```

NOTE: Obviously Chaucer did not write a book with this title; therefore this entry is correct for this book. If you quoted the introduction by Dr. Hopper, you would use this card for bibliography and for footnote. If you quoted the lines from Chaucer with the older spelling, your card would be thus:

16a.

```
Chaucer, Geoffrey.
"The Pardoner's Tale."
Chaucer's Canterbury Tales: An Interlinear
  Translation.
Ed. and trans. Vincent F. Hopper.
Woodbury: Barron's,
1970. Print.
```

17. an edition subsequent to the first edition

```
Coe, Michael D.
The Maya, 5th ed.
New York: Thames and Hudson,
1993. Print.
```

18. a modern reprint of an older edition

```
Toor, Frances.
Mexican Popular Arts.
1939;
rpt. Detroit: Blaine Ethridge Books,
1973. Print.
```

19. a pamphlet, bulletin, manual, or monograph

```
Mulryan, Lenore H.
Mexican Figural Ceramists and Their
  Work (Monograph Series, no. 16).
Los Angeles: Museum of Cultural History,
  U of California, Los Angeles,
1982. Print.
```

NOTE: Omit parenthetical entry if the work is not one of a series.

20. a catalog of an exhibition

Billeter, Erika, ed.
The Blue House: The World of Frida Kahlo (an exhibit
  at the Schirn Kunsthalle, Frankfurt, March 6-May
  23, 1993 and The Museum of Fine Arts, Houston, June
  6-August 29, 1993).
Frankfurt: Schirn Kunsthalle and Houston: Museum of
  Fine Arts,
1993. Print.

21. a government document

U. S., Congressional Record.
80th Cong., 2nd Sess., 1948.
XCII, Part 6, 5539. Print.

22. a dictionary

Webster's New Collegiate Dictionary.
Springfield: G. & C.
  Merriam Company,
1984. Print.

PRINT MEDIA

FORM FOR A SOURCE CONTAINED WITHIN A LARGER WORK

Jay, Gregory S.
"Knowledge, Power, and the Struggle for
  Representation."
College English January 1994:
9-29. Print.

1st line: author's name in inverted order
(For two or more authors, see examples 3, 4, and 5 in the preceding section.)

end punctuation: period

2nd line: title of the article, essay, story, or poem (the contained work) enclosed in quotation marks
(The title is capitalized except for CAPs—short conjunctions, articles, and short prepositions.)

end punctuation: period before the closing quotation marks unless there is punctuation at that point as part of the title, in which case that punctuation is retained inside the quotation mark, and your period is omitted

3rd line: title of the larger work in which the article appears followed by the date of publication with the date first, if one is given, followed by the month and then the year, thus: 7 January 1994.
NOTE: Some authorities distinguish between popular periodicals appearing weekly, biweekly, monthly, or bimonthly and scholarly journals, which are generally quarterly publications. When such a distinction is made, popular periodicals are referred to using the form above while scholarly journals are referred to by substituting the volume and issue number and the year of publication for the date in the 3rd line, thus: College English 56.1 (1994)

end punctuation: colon

4th line: the pages on which the particular work can be found and the medium of publication
(The abbreviations p. or pp. are not used. To give the pages on which a work occurs, use, for example:
9 to indicate that the work is complete on page 9;
9–29 to indicate that the work covers those twenty-one pages;
9–29, 84 to indicate that after the first twenty-one pages, the work concludes on page 84.
9–29, 84–86 to indicate that after the first twenty-one pages, the work continues from pages 84 to 86.)

end punctuation: period. The page numbers are followed by a period and the medium of publication.

PRINT MEDIA

MODELS FOR A SOURCE CONTAINED WITHIN A LARGER WORK

1. the basic form

```
Jay, Gregory S.
"Knowledge, Power, and the Struggle for Representa-
   tion."
College English January 1994:
9-29. Print.
```

2. a periodical article with no author

```
"The Presidential Policy Scoreboard."
The World and I June 1988:
52-55. Print.
```

3. a titled book review

```
Paz, Octavio.
"Food of the Gods."
Trans. Eliot Weinberger.
Review of The Blood of Kings by Linda
   Schele and Mary Ellen Miller.
The New York Review of Books 26 February 1987:
3-7. Print.
```

4. an untitled book review

```
Neumann, Franke J.
Review of Masks of the Spirit: Image and Metaphor in
   Mesoamerica by Peter T. Markman and Roberta H.
   Markman.
Religious Studies Review April 1993:
179. Print.
```

5. a newspaper article or editorial

```
Williams, Dan.
"400-Year Church Ties Cut by Ancient Mexican
  Tribe."
Los Angeles Times 5 July 1987:
I:1, 12-13. Print.
```

NOTE: On the last line you must indicate the section (I in this case) in which the article appears as well as the page numbers. If there are various editions of the newspaper (Eastern Edition, Late Edition, and National Edition), you should specify the particular edition you are using after the date on line 3.

6. an essay (or other work) written by one person in an anthology edited by another

```
Eliade, Mircea.
"The Symbolism of Shadows in Archaic Religions."
Symbolism, the Sacred, and the Arts.
Ed. Diane Apostolos-Cappadona.
New York: Crossroad,
1988.
3-16. Print.
```

7. an encyclopedia article

```
Bolle, Kees W.
"Myth and Mythology: The Nature, Functions, and
  Types of Myth."
The New Encyclopaedia Britannica: Macropaedia.
15th ed. 1986.
24: 710-720. Print.
```

NOTE: Most articles are signed with only the initials of the author; at the front of the first volume is a list of the initials and full names of the contributors.

For an unsigned article, you would write nothing on the first line above the title of the article; leave the line blank because you may find the name of the author later.

Encyclopedias reverse titles and names in order to list articles alphabetically; you may or may not, but be consistent.

8. an introduction or limited part of a book by one other than the author

```
Campbell, Joseph.
"Introduction."
Masks of the Spirit: Image and Metaphor
  in Mesoamerica.
Peter T. Markman and Roberta H. Markman.
Berkeley: U of California P,
1989.
ix-xix. Print.
```

9. author of a work in a book in a series edited by others

```
Waardenburg, Jacques.
"Symbolic Aspects of Myth."
Myth, Symbol, and Reality.
Ed. Alan M. Olson.
Vol. 1 of The Boston University Studies in
  Philosophy and Religion.
Ed. Leroy S. Rouner.
Notre Dame: U of Notre Dame P,
1980.
41-68. Print.
```

10. a reprint with critical comment by the editor

```
Wright, Andrew.
"Afterword."
Joyce Cary. The Horse's Mouth.
1944;
rpt. New York: Harper & Row Perennial Library,
1965.
347-353. Print.
```

11. a casebook (a text for controlled research)

```
Stevenson, David.
"J. D. Salinger: The Mirror of Crisis."
The Nation 9 March 1957:
215-217;
rpt. If You Really Want to Know: A Catcher
  Casebook.
Ed. Malcolm M. Marsden.
Chicago: Scott, Foresman,
1963.
22-25. Print.
```

NOTE: There are two ways to use a casebook: as an anthology of essays about a particular subject or as a library containing essays, which you will read and document as if you were reading the original. For the latter use, the original pagination appears in the casebook with slash marks wherever a page change occurred in the original. Check with your instructor about how to use the casebook; but it would never be wrong to use this model form.

PRINT MEDIA

FORMS FOR SPECIAL PROBLEMS

1. an interview

```
Markman, Roberta H.
Professor of Comparative Literature,
  California State U, Long Beach.
Personal interview on Mexican masks.
Long Beach, California,
April 16, 1994.
```

NOTE: Unless the person interviewed is well known, you should indicate through the use of the person's title why he or she is an authority on the subject of the interview.

2. an unpublished lecture

```
Markman, Peter T.
Professor of English, Fullerton College.
Class Lecture on Carlos Fuentes, The
  Death of Artemio Cruz.
Fullerton, California,
May 3, 1992.
```

3. a published lecture

```
Vonnegut, Kurt, Jr.
"Address to Graduating Class at Bennington
  College, 1970."
Wampeters, Foma and Granfalloons (Opinions).
New York: Dell,
1976.
159-168. Print.
```

4. photocopied material

```
Brown, Betty Ann.
"Fiestas de Oaxaca."
1977. Photocopy.
```

NOTE: Try to give as much identifying information as you can for
       material of this nature.

5. an unpublished thesis or dissertation

```
Markman, Roberta H.
"Mann's Joseph: From Dreamer to Artist."
Diss. Occidental College, Los Angeles,
1969. Print.
```

6. a letter

```
Hemingway, Ernest.
A letter to Roberta Hoffman, dated August 12,
   1957, New York, and now in the archives of
   U of Texas at El Paso Library,
   El Paso, Texas. Print.
```

NOTE: In a footnote, simply: Unpublished letter from Ernest Heming-
          way to Roberta Hoffman, August 12, 1957.

7. the Bible or any well-known literary work that can be identified by book or scene plus lines or by chapter and verse

```
I Corinthians.
The Bible.
Revised Standard Version. Print.
```

NOTE: The names of sacred scripture are neither underlined nor put
          in quotation marks. The translation of the Bible is assumed to
          be the King James Version unless another is named, as in the
          preceding example.

```
Milton, John.
Paradise Lost.
Book 1. Print.
```

NOTE: The particular edition you used is not needed unless the work
          is a translation.

          The name of a novel, a play, or a long poem would be under-
          lined even if it is part of an anthology.

8. an abridgment

```
Style Manual (abridged), rev. ed.
Washington, D.C.: Government Printing Office,
1984. Print.
```

9. record jacket notes

```
Mahler, Gustav.
Symphony No. 4.
Concertgebouw Orchestra, Amsterdam.
Cond. Bernard Haitink.
Philips, SAL 3729 802 888 LY.
Jacket notes. Print.
```

10. a pamphlet included with a record or compact disc

```
Kostelanetz, Richard, and Editors of
  Time-Life Records.
"A Listener's Guide to the Recordings."
The Music of Today.
In The Story of Great Music series.
Time-Life Records, STL 145. Print.
```

ELECTRONIC MEDIA

FORM FOR A SOURCE THAT IS NOT PART OF A LARGER WORK

(Note: You need not have used or read the entire work.)

```
Ashliman, D. L., ed. and trans.
Folklore and Mythology Electronic Texts.
1996-2000, U of Pittsburgh. Web.
1 January 2001 <http://www.pitt.edu/~dash/folktexts.html>.
```

1st line: author's or editor's name in inverted order

(If there is both an author and an editor or translator, the author's name goes on the first line, and the editor's name goes on a third line in normal order after the title, as in example 4.)

end punctuation: period

2nd line: title of source
  (Capitalize the first and last word and all other words except CAPS—
  short conjunctions, articles, and short prepositions; underline each
  word separately to indicate title; underlining is a substitute for italics.)
  end punctuation: period

3rd line: facts of publication and medium of publication
  (Electronic media do not always provide complete facts of publication so you must indicate here the information given in your particular source. A complete entry would provide, in this order, the
  version number if it is not included in the title, the date of electronic
  publication or of the latest update, and the name of the sponsoring
  institution. If the source is also available in print form, place the facts
  of publication of the print version in parentheses after the facts of
  publication of the electronic version on this line, as in example 4.)
  end punctuation: period

4th line: date of access and electronic address
  (Since Internet sites are changed frequently, it is important to
  indicate when you accessed the site. The address is enclosed in
  angle brackets to indicate precisely what is included because you
  must type the address *exactly* into your computer in order to
  access the site. For that reason, it is imperative that you be accurate here. If the address must be divided between two lines, try
  to break it after a slash or similar symbol; do *not* allow your word
  processing program to place a hyphen at this dividing point.)
  end punctuation: period.

ELECTRONIC MEDIA

MODELS FOR A SOURCE THAT IS NOT PART OF A LARGER WORK

1. the basic form

```
Ashliman, D. L., ed. and trans.
Folklore and Mythology Electronic Texts.
1996-2000, U of Pittsburgh. Web.
1 January 2001 <http://www.pitt.edu/~dash/folktexts.html>.
```

2. online information database

```
Crane, Gregory, ed.
The Perseus Digital Library.
Tufts U. Web.
3 January 2001 <http://www.perseus.tufts.edu/
indexplain.html>.
```

3. Internet site maintained by an individual or group

```
Sherwood School Students.
Building the Windy City. Web.
27 December 2000 <http://library.thinkquest.org/
j002846>.
```

NOTE: There are often no facts of publication for an Internet site of this type.

4. online book (with an author and a translator)

```
Euripides.
Alcestis.
Trans. David Kovacs.
The Perseus Digital Library. Tufts U (Cambridge,
MA: Harvard U P, in press). Web.
26 December 2000 <http://www.perseus.tufts.edu/
cgi-bin/ptext?doc=perseus%3atext%3a1999.01.0088>.
```

NOTE: Often online books, as in this case, are also available in print form. Place the facts of publication of the print version in parentheses after the facts of publication of the electronic version.

5. e-mail from a source to you

```
Colina, Armando, Director, Galeria Arvil, Mexico
City <colina@conecta.com.mx>.
Re Frida, e-mail to Peter T. Markman.
12 December 2000.
```

NOTE: The first line gives the author's title to indicate his authority on the subject and his e-mail address.

6. posting to an electronic bulletin board or discussion group

```
Poirier, L.
This Site.
11 June 1999, Genesis Discussion. Web.
29 December 2000 <http://library.thinkquest.org/
    29064/cgi-bin/ultraboard/ultraboard.pl?action=
    showpost&board=feed&post=1&idle=7&sort=0&order=
    descend&page=)&session=>.
```

ELECTRONIC MEDIA

FORM FOR A SOURCE CONTAINED WITHIN A LARGER WORK

```
Ryan, Susan M.
"Melville, Race, and the Ambiguities of Violence."
American Literary History Winter 2000. Web.
22 December 2000 <http://muse.jhu.edu/journals/alh/
joc/alh12.4.html>.
```

1st line: author's name in inverted order
    end punctuation: period

2nd line: title of the article, essay, story, or poem (the contained work) enclosed in quotation marks

(The title is capitalized except for CAPS—short conjunctions, articles, and short prepositions.)

end punctuation: period before the closing quotation marks unless there is punctuation at that point as part of the title, in which case that punctuation is retained inside the quotation mark, and your period is omitted

3rd line: title of the larger work in which the article appears followed by the date of publication with the date first, if one is given, followed by the month and then the year, thus: 15 November 2000 and the medium of publication

NOTE: Some authorities distinguish between popular periodicals appearing weekly, biweekly, monthly, or bimonthly and scholarly journals, such as the one in this example, which are generally quarterly publications. When such a distinction is made, popular periodicals are referred to using the form above while scholarly journals are referred to by substituting the volume and issue number and the year of publication in parentheses for the date in the third line, thus: *American Literary History* 12.4 (2000).

end punctuation: period

4th line: date of access and electronic address

(Since Internet sites are changed frequently, it is important to indicate when you accessed the site. The address is enclosed in angle brackets to indicate precisely what is included because you must type the address *exactly* into your computer in order to access the site. For that reason it is imperative that you be accurate here. If the address must be divided between two lines, try to break it after a slash or similar symbol; do *not* allow your word processing program to place a hyphen at this dividing point.)

end punctuation: period.

ELECTRONIC MEDIA

MODELS FOR A SOURCE CONTAINED WITHIN A LARGER WORK

1. the basic form

Ryan, Susan M.
"Melville, Race, and the Ambiguities of Violence."
American Literary History Winter 2000. Web.
22 December 2000 ⟨*http://muse.jhu.edu/journals/alh/ joc/alh12.4.html*⟩.

2. an article in an online periodical

Chamberlain, Daniel.
"Bookmarks: Less Is More."
Themestream 30 September 2000. Web.
7 December 2000 ⟨*http://www.themestream.com/ gspd_browse/browse/view_article.gsp?c_id=195850&id_ list=&cookied=t*⟩.

3. a book review

Gorra, Michael.
"After the Fall."
Review of Disgrace by J. M. Coetzee.
The New York Times on the Web 28 November 1999.
Web.
6 December 2000 ⟨*http://www.nytimes.com/books/99/ 11/28/reviews/99128.28gorrat.html*⟩.

4. a newspaper article or editorial

Coetzee, J. M.
"Into the Dark Chamber: The Novelist and South Africa."
The New York Times on the Web 12 January 1986. Web.
29 December 2000 ⟨*http://www.nytimes.com/books/97/ 11/02/home/coetzee-chamber.html*⟩.

5. a work written by one person in an anthology, edited by another

Andersen, Hans Christian.
"Yggdrasil."
<u>Folklore</u> and <u>Mythology</u> <u>Electronic</u> <u>Texts</u>.
Ed. and trans. D. L. Ashliman.
1996-2000, U of Pittsburgh. Web.
3 December 2000 ⟨*http://www.pitt.edu/~dash/ yggdrasil.html*⟩.

6. an encyclopedia article

"Whitman."
<u>The</u> <u>Cambridge</u> <u>History</u> <u>of</u> <u>English</u> <u>and</u> <u>American</u> <u>Literature</u> <u>in</u> <u>18</u> <u>Volumes</u>.
1907-1921.
Vol. 16. Web.
2 January 2001 ⟨*http://www.bartleby.com/226/1607.html*⟩.

ELECTRONIC MEDIA

FORMS FOR SPECIAL PROBLEMS

1. a CD-ROM or DVD

<u>Perseus</u> <u>2.0</u>: <u>Interactive</u> <u>Sources</u> <u>and</u> <u>Studies</u> <u>on</u> <u>Ancient</u> <u>Greece</u>.
New Haven: Yale UP, 1996.
CD-ROM. 4 discs.

NOTE: To cite a work contained on a CD-ROM, place the author's name, in inverted order, on the first line and the title of the contained work on the second line as in the basic form for a source contained within a larger work.

2. a record, audiotape, or compact disc

```
Brahms, Johannes.
Violin Sonatas Nos. 1-3.
Itzhak Perlman, violin, and Vladimir Ashkenazy,
  piano.
EMI/Angel, CDC 7 47403 2
Compact Disc.
```

3. a film, videotape, or DVD

```
Wings of Desire.
Dir. Wim Wenders.
Orion Pictures Corp.,
1988. Film.
```

4. a lecture on a record, tape, or compact disc

```
Scherman, Thomas, narrator.
"Musical Program Notes."
Beethoven's Symphony No. 5 in C Minor, Op. 67.
The Philharmonic Promenade Orchestra of London.
Cond. Sir Adrian Boult.
Vanguard, MARS 3005. LP.
```

5. a radio program

```
Tribute: Ernest von Dohanyi.
KFAC (1330 AM, 92.3 FM), Los Angeles
7-8 pm., 26 July 1998. Radio.
```

6. a television program

```
Moyers: Joseph Campbell and the Power of Myth, pt. 1.
KCET (Channel 28), Los Angeles. PBS.
10-11 pm., 23 May 1998. TV.
```

7. computer software

```
Weyh, John A., Joseph R. Crook, and Les N. Hauge.
The Mole Concept.
Pt. 2 of Concepts in General Chemistry.
IBM PC Computer software.
COMPress.
```

HOW TO PREPARE
THE FINAL BIBLIOGRAPHY
(TO BE DONE AS PART OF STEP 10)

1. Take out all the bibliography cards to which you have referred in your footnotes. These cards constitute your working bibliography and are the only ones that will be used in making your final bibliography.

2. The number of sources you will list on the final bibliography should equal the number of sources used in your paper.

3. Alphabetize your working bibliography cards according to the first letter that appears on the card, excepting *a*, *an*, and *the*. (The first letter may be in the author's name, the title of a magazine article, and so forth.) If the title begins with a Roman numeral, alphabetize according to the word that follows the Roman numeral; if the first word in the title is an Arabic number, alphabetize according to the way that number would be spelled. For example, "X Steps" would be alphabetized under *S*, but "10 Steps" would be alphabetized under *T*.

4. Since the bibliography page is a title page, the title, "Works Cited," is centered and typed in capitals without underlining, and the page number is centered at the bottom of the page. "Works Cited" is now the preferred title for this page, in part because it probably contains a number of works other than books. However, if you include works that you have not cited in the paper, this page may be entitled "Works Consulted" or "Bibliography."

5. The bibliography entries are single-spaced within each entry and double-spaced between entries. Write as a continuous sentence; do not divide into lines as on the cards. The second and subse-

quent lines of each entry are indented as for a paragraph (five spaces); the punctuation on the bibliography card is copied exactly.

6. Bibliography entries are never numbered (except in the CSE format). Ordinarily, the bibliography is not divided into types of sources.

NOTE: There are many accepted styles for bibliographical citations. The four most popularly accepted ones being MLA (*MLA Handbook for Writers of Research Papers*, 2009) used primarily in the humanities, APA (*Publication Manual of the American Psychological Association*, 2010) used primarily in the social sciences, CSE (*Scientific Style and Format: The CSE Manual for Authors, Editors, and Publishers*, 2006) used primarily in the sciences, and Chicago (*The Chicago Manual of Style*, 2010). The first three (MLA, APA, and CSE) all use parenthetical references in the text of the paper to refer to items in the bibliography. Chicago continues to use the more traditional method of footnote or endnote references. We will present the Chicago format for footnotes, bibliography, and a sample paper using them in an appendix (pp. 125 to 149).

There are also other formats that are acceptable in particular disciplines. Manuals of style published for many of the disciplines explain and illustrate the different formats preferred by scholars in the various areas. A list of some of the most widely used can be found on pp. 157 to 159. It might be wise to check with your instructor regarding the preferred form for your paper if there is a specialized form preferred. However, the most important point to remember is that it is essential to be consistent; use one or the other style throughout a single piece of work. The following section is based on the MLA style format, but see pp. 58 to 59 for a brief discussion of the other formats.

WORKS CITED*

Andersen, Hans Christian. "Yggdrasil." Folklore and Mythology Electronic Texts. Ed. and trans. D. L. Ashliman. 1996-2000, U of Pittsburgh. Web. 3 December 2000 <*http://www.pitt.edu/~dash/yggdr sil.html*>.

Apostolos-Cappadona, Diane, ed. *Symbolism, the Sacred, and the Arts*. New York: Crossroad, 1988. Print.

Ashliman, D. L., ed. and trans. *Folklore and Mythology Electronic Texts*. 1996-2000, U of Pittsburgh. Web. 1 January 2001 <*http://www.pitt.edu/ ~dash/folktexts.html*>.

Billeter, Erika, ed. *The Blue House: The World of Frida Kahlo* (an exhibit at the Schirn Kunsthalle, Frankfurt, March 6-May 23, 1993 and The Museum of Fine Arts, Houston, June 6-August 29, 1993). Frankfurt: Schirn Kunsthalle and Houston: Museum of Fine Arts, 1993. Print.

Bolle, Kees W. "Myth and Mythology: The Nature, Functions, and Types of Myth." *The New Encyclopaedia Britannica: Macropaedia*. 15th ed. 1986. 24: 710-720. Print.

Brahms, Johannes. *Violin Sonatas Nos. 1-3*. Itzhak Perlman, violin, and Vladimir Ashkenazy, piano. EMI/Angel, CDC 7 47403 2. Compact disc.

NOTE: All of these sources are reproduced as footnotes beginning on p. 126.

---

*This is a sample Works Cited page compiled from the sample bibliography cards shown on the preceding pages.

Broda, Johanna, David Carrasco, and Eduardo Matos Moctezuma. *The Great Temple of Tenochtitlan: Center and Periphery in the Aztec World*. Berkeley: U of California P, 1987. Print.

Brown, Betty Ann. "Fiestas de Oaxaca." 1977 Photocopy.

Budge, E. A. Wallis. *The Gods of the Egyptians or Studies in Egyptian Mythology*. 2 vols. 1904; rpt. New York: Dover Publications, 1969. Vol. 2. Print.

Campbell, Joseph. *The Inner Reaches of Outer Space: Metaphor as Myth and as Religion*. New York: Alfred van der Marck Editions, 1986. Print.

[†]---. "Introduction." *Masks of the Spirit: Image and Metaphor in Mesoamerica*. Peter T. Markman and Roberta H. Markman. Berkeley: U of California P, 1989. ix-xix. Print.

---. *The Power of Myth* with Bill Moyers. Ed. Betty Sue Flowers. New York: Doubleday, 1988. Print.

Chamberlain, Daniel. "Bookmarks: Less Is More." *Themestream* Web. 30 September 2000. 7 December 2000 〈*http://www.themestream.com/gspd_browse/browse/view_article.gsp?c_id=195850&id_list=&cookied=t*〉.

Chaucer, Geoffrey. "The Pardoner's Tale." *Chaucer's Canterbury Tales: An Interlinear Translation*. Ed. and trans. Vincent F. Hopper. Woodbury, New York: Barron's, 1970. Print.

[†]These three hyphens followed by a period indicate that the author for this entry is the same as the author for the entry immediately above. Note, however, that hyphens are not used when the author is joined by another as in the following Coe entries.

Coe, Michael D. *The Maya*. 5th ed. New York: Thames and Hudson, 1993. Print.

Coe, Michael D., and Richard A. Diehl. *The People of the River*. Vol. 2 of *In the Land of the Olmec*. 2 vols. Austin: U of Texas P, 1980. Print.

Coetzee, J. M. "Into the Dark Chamber: The Novelist and South Africa." *The New York Times on the Web* Web. 12 January 1986. 29 December 2000 <*http://www.nytimes.com/books/97/11/02/home/ coetzee-chamber.html*>.

Colina, Armando, Director, Galeria Arvil, Mexico City <*colina@conecta.com.mx*>. *Re Frida*, e-mail to Peter T. Markman. 12 December 2000.

Crane, Gregory, ed. *The Perseus Digital Library*. Tufts University. Web. 3 January 2001 <*http://www. perseus.tufts.edu/indexplain.html*>.

I Corinthians. The Bible. Revised Standard Version.

Eliade, Mircea. *Images and Symbols*. Trans. Philip Mairet. Kansas City: Sheed Andrews and McMeel, 1961. Print.

---. "The Symbolism of Shadows in Archaic Religions." *Symbolism, the Sacred, and the Arts*. Ed. Diane Apostolos-Cappadona. New York: Crossroad, 1988. 3-16. Print.

Euripides. *Alcestis*. Trans. David Kovacs. The Perseus Digital Library. Tufts U (Cambridge, MA: Harvard U P, in press.). Web. 26 December 2000 <*http://www.perseus.tufts.edu/cgi-bin/ptext? doc=perseus%3atext%3a1999.01.0088*>.

Gorra, Michael. "After the Fall." Review of *Disgrace* by J. M. Coetzee. *The New York Times on the Web* Web. 28 November 1999. 6 December 2000 <*http://www.nytimes.com/books/99/11/28/reviews/991 28.28gorrat.html*>.

Hemingway, Ernest. A letter to Roberta Hoffman, dated August 12, 1957, New York, and now in the archives of U of Texas at El Paso Library, El Paso, Texas.

Hopper, Vincent F., ed. and trans. *Chaucer's Canterbury Tales: An Interlinear Translation*. Woodbury, New York: Barron's, 1970. Print.

Instituto Guerrerense de la Cultura. *Calendario Fiestas del Estado de Guerrero*. Chilpancingo, Guerrero, México: Instituto Guerrerense de la Cultura, 1987. Print.

Jay, Gregory S. "Knowledge, Power, and the Struggle for Representation." *College English* January 1994: 9-29. Print.

Kostelanetz, Richard, and Editors of Time-Life Records. "A Listener's Guide to the Recordings." *The Music of Today*. In *The Story of Great Music* series. Time-Life Records, STL 145. Print.

Lothrop, Samuel K., and others. *Essays in Pre-Columbian Art and Archaeology*. Cambridge: Harvard UP, 1961. Print.

Maclagen, David. *Creation Myths: Man's Introduction to the World*. In the *Art and Imagination* series. Ed. Jill Purce. London: Thames and Hudson, 1977. Print.

Mahler, Gustav. *Symphony No. 4.* Concertgebouw Orchestra, Amsterdam. Cond. Bernard Haitink. Philips, SAL 3729 802 888 LY. Jacket notes.

Markman, Peter T. Professor of English, Fullerton College. Class Lecture on Carlos Fuentes, *The Death of Artemio Cruz.* Fullerton College, Fullerton, California. 3 May 1988.

Markman, Roberta H., and Peter T. Markman. *The Flayed God. The Mesoamerican Mythological Tradition.* San Francisco: Harper San Francisco, 1992. Print.

Markman, Roberta H. "Mann's Joseph: From Dreamer to Artist." Diss. Occidental College, Los Angeles. 1969. Print.

---. Professor of Comparative Literature, California State U, Long Beach. Personal interview on Mexican masks. Long Beach, California. 16 April 1988.

Máscaras Mexicanas: *de la Colección del Ing. Victor José Moya.* México: Dirección de Museos del Instituto Nacional de Antropología e Historia. 1974. Print.

Milton, John. *Paradise Lost.* Book 1. Print.

Moyers: Joseph Campbell and the Power of Myth, pt. 1. KCET (Channel 28), Los Angeles. PBS. 10-11 p.m., 23 May 1998.

Mulryan, Lenore H. *Mexican Figural Ceramists and Their Work* (Monograph Series, no. 16). Los Angeles: Museum of Cultural History, U of California, Los Angeles, 1982. Print.

Muser, Curt. comp. *Facts and Artifacts of Ancient Middle America.* New York: E. P. Dutton, 1978. Print.

Neruda, Pablo. *A New Decade (Poems: 1958-1967)* Ed. Ben Belitt. Trans. Ben Belitt and Alastair Reid. New York: Grove Press, 1969. Print.

Neumann, Franke J. Review of *Masks of the Spirit: Image and Metaphor in Mesoamerica* by Peter T. Markman and Roberta H. Markman. *Religious Studies Review* April 1993: 179. Print.

Paz, Octavio. "Food of the Gods." Trans. Eliot Weinberger. Review of *The Blood of Kings* by Linda Schele and Mary Ellen Miller. *The New York Review Of Books* 26 February 1987: 3-7. Print.

Perseus 2.0: Interactive Sources and Studies on Ancient Greece. New Haven: Yale UP, 1996. CD-ROM. 4 discs.

Poirier, L. *This Site*. 11 June 1999, Genesis Discussion. Web. 29 December 2000 <*http://library.thinkquest. org/29064/cgi-bin/ultraboard/ultraboard. pl?action=showpost&board=feed&post=1&idle=7 &sort=0&order=descend&page=)&session=*>.

"The Presidential Policy Scoreboard." *The World and I* June 1988: 52-55. Print.

Ryan, Susan M. "Melville, Race, and the Ambiguities of Violence." *American Literary History* Winter 2000. Web. 22 December 2000 <*http://muse.jhu.edu/ journals/alh/joc/alh12.4.html*>.

Scherman, Thomas, narrator and cond. "Musical Program Notes." Beethoven's *Symphony No. 5 in C Minor, Op. 67*. The Philharmonic Promenade Orchestra of London. Cond. Sir Adrian Boult. Vanguard, MARS 3005. LP.

Sherwood School Students. *Building the Windy City.* Web. 27 December 2000 <*http://library.thinkquest. org/ j002846*>.

Stevenson, David. "J. D. Salinger: The Mirror of Crisis." *The Nation* 9 March 1957: 215-217; rpt. *If You Really Want to Know: A Catcher Casebook.* Ed. Malcolm M. Marsden. Chicago: Scott, Foresman, 1963. 22-25. Print.

Style Manual (abridged), rev. ed. Washington, D.C.: Government Printing Office, 1984. Print.

Sullivan, Thelma D., trans. *A Scattering of Jades: Stories, Poems, and Prayers of the Aztecs.* Ed. T. J. Knab. New York: Simon and Schuster, 1994. Print.

Toor, Francis. *Mexican Popular Arts.* 1939; rpt. Detroit: Blaine Ethridge Books, 1973. Print.

Tribute: Ernest von Dohnanyi. KFAC (1330 AM, 92.3 FM), Los Angeles. 7-8 p.m., 26 July 1998.

U.S. Congressional Record. 80th Cong., 2nd Sess. 1948. XCII, Pt. 6, 5539. Print.

Vonnegut, Kurt, Jr. "Address to Graduating Class at Bennington College, 1970." *Wampeters, Foma and Granfalloons (Opinions).* New York: Dell, 1976. 159-168. Print.

Waardenburg, Jacques. "Symbolic Aspects of Myth." *Myth, Symbol, and Reality.* Ed. Alan M. Olson. Vol. 1 of The Boston University Studies in Philosophy and Religion. Ed. Leroy S. Rouner. Notre Dame, Indiana: U of Notre Dame P, 1980. 41-68. Print.

Webster's New Collegiate Dictionary. Springfield, Massachusetts: G. & C. Merriam Company, 1984. Print.

Weyh, John A., Joseph R. Crook, and Les N. Hauge. *The Mole Concept*. Pt. 2 of *Concepts in General Chemistry*. IBM PC Computer software. COMPress.

"Whitman." *The Cambridge History of English and American Literature in 18 Volumes*. 1907-1921. Vol. 16. Web. 2 January 2001 ⟨*http://www.bartleby.com/226/ 1607.html*⟩.

Williams, Dan. "400-Year Church Ties Cut by Ancient Mexican Tribe." *Los Angeles Times* 5 July 1987: I:1, 12-13. Print.

Wings of Desire. Dir. Wim Wenders. Orion Pictures Corp., 1988. Film.

Wright, Andrew. "Afterword." Joyce Cary. *The Horse's Mouth*. 1944; rpt. New York: Harper & Row/Perennial Library, 1965. 347-353. Print.

AUTHOR-DATE SYSTEM (USED PRIMARILY IN THE SOCIAL AND NATURAL SCIENCES)

In the author-date style both the bibliographical form and the form for citing the source in the text differ from the MLA style illustrated previously. The following discussion is designed to provide only basic information about the APA system. If you intend to use this system, consult *Publication Manual of the American Psychological Association*, 6th ed. Washington, D.C.: American Psychological Association, 2010. The CSE author-date system is similar. If you intend to use the CSE system, see *Scientific Style and Format: The CSE Manual for Authors, Editors, and Publishers*, 7th ed. Wheat Ridge: Council of Science Editors, 2010.

FORM FOR BIBLIOGRAPHY USING THE AUTHOR-DATE SYSTEM

The appropriate title for the page is "References." For a book or article with one author, this format requires that you cite only the initials of the author's first name and capitalize only the first word of the title and subtitle. The year of publication is placed immediately following the author's name:

Campbell, J. (1986). *The inner reaches of outer space: Metaphor as myth and as religion*. New York: Alfred van der Marck Editions.

Jay, G. (1994). Knowledge, power, and the struggle for representation. *College English*, 56, 9–29.

For a second book by the same author, the name is repeated.

For a book with two authors, invert the surnames of both authors and separate the names with a comma followed by &.

Markman, R., & Markman, P. (1992). *The flayed god: The Mesoamerican mythological tradition*. San Francisco: Harper San Francisco.

See the following item #4 for the form of reference lists in which there are many works by the same author(s).

The major differences between the author-date system and MLA styles can be summarized as follows:

1. Author-date entries substitute initials for the first names of authors or editors, whereas MLA style cites first names.

2. Author-date style capitalizes only the first word of a book or article title or subtitle and proper names, and article titles are not placed in quotes, whereas in MLA style all major words in titles are capitalized and article titles are enclosed in quotation marks. Both capitalize journal titles.

3. In citing dates, author-date format places the date after the author's name whereas in MLA style, the dates are placed with information about publication.

FORM FOR PARENTHETICAL DOCUMENTATION USING THE AUTHOR-DATE SYSTEM

Parenthetical reference notes for the author-date style include the author's last name and the year of publication followed by a comma and a page reference: (Campbell 1987, p. 60). If any of this information is given in the text, it may be omitted from the parenthetical reference. If two or more works by the same author were published in the same year, each is identified by a lowercase letter: 1987a and 1987b; a short title to distinguish between the works is not used.

(See pp. 91 to 93 for a discussion of parenthetical references using the MLA style-format.)

STEP

TAKE NOTES FROM RELEVANT SOURCES

At the heart of any research project is the gathering of information. The success of the project will be largely the result of the quality and quantity of that information. But to be useful, that information must be gathered and recorded in a way that will make it easy to handle when the information-gathering phase of the project is completed and the organizing phase begins. The traditional way of accomplishing this is to record each piece of information on a notecard, usually a 4 × 6-inch index card, along with an indication of the source of that information. This method allows you the freedom later to assemble the separate pieces of information in the order that you will use them in your paper, rather than having your notes fixed in the order they were found in the original works.

Much research now, however, is done with the use of a computer, and the notes taken will thus exist as integral parts of a computer file or as items on a printout. The problem, of course, is that you will not use the items in the order in which they now exist in the computer file or the printout, and thus they may be more difficult to handle than individual notecards that can be sorted and reassembled in the order in which you will use them. This problem may be solved in a number of ways. The most obvious solution would be simply to leave sufficient space between each of the notes as you take them so you can print them out and then separate them with scissors, thereby creating note-cards. Or if you carefully label each note with a key word or label as described below, you will be able to use your computer's "find" function to gather the "cards," or notes that go together and then reassemble them by cutting and pasting. In addition, there are computer programs that will allow you to make something similar to traditional notecards on your computer. Microsoft Word has a "Stickies" application that can easily be adapted to note-taking, Google offers "Google Notes," and there are a number of database programs that may be adapted to note-taking (after all, what you would be creating with your paper notecards is, in computer terms, a database). Finally, there are programs—such as Endnote and Evernote, for example—that are designed to facilitate the use of your computer for this type of research. Using your computer in one of these ways has the advantage of allowing you to cut and paste information into your paper once you have organized it, rather than having to retype it.

It is interesting to note that computer programs designed for research writing are based exactly on the traditional method of taking and using notes, so there is no real conflict between the older and newer techniques. We will present the traditional method of note-taking here in Step 5 as a model for the basic process researchers have always used, indicating along the way how it can be modified for computer use. You may well discover other ways to adapt the method to your own computer use. After all, it is not the specifics of the method that are most important, but the basic process. That is to say, what is important is the process of gathering information so that it is readily available for you when it comes time to organize your information. When you begin the writing process, you don't want to be stuck hunting for the correct information to use in your paper, or worse, end up forgetting useful information or citing your sources incorrectly. Using notecards not only keeps a record of the information that you find important in an easy and manageable form, but it allows you the opportunity to save the information you don't use immediately for use in a project later on. During the writing process, it is not uncommon to find yourself wanting to use a piece of information that was more important than you originally thought and vice versa. As you progress through the ten steps of writing your research paper, you'll be glad you have a reliable "database" of information right at your fingertips. It is probably best, though, to use one method throughout the note-taking process rather than having some notes on your computer, some on notecards, and some on random pieces of paper. A uniform system will make it much easier for you when it comes time to assemble and use your notes.

As we have just noted, the order in which you take notes will not be the order in which you will use them in your paper; therefore, it is important to keep them independent of each other and clear in meaning to you. Each notecard must be precisely identified as to source and page so that you can document the information if you use it in your paper; or if you are working with sources that are not printed matter, be sure to indicate how and where you obtained your information.

There are times when you will need to use information from a periodical or a book that does not circulate and you may not have time to take all the notes that would be valuable to you. You might find it helpful to photocopy material to reread and work with at home. Be sure that you (1) make a copy of the title page and copyright page for a book and the publication-data page of a periodical and staple it to the material you copy and (2) that you do not cut off the page numbers as you copy them. At some point you should enter the relevant information on a bibliography card. Similarly, if you download articles or portions of longer works from Internet sources, be sure the download includes all the information regarding the Web address that you will need for your Works Cited page (see pp. 40 to 48), and record that information on a bibliography card.

The amount and kind of information you write on each card will vary with the type of note you take, which will be guided not only by the information you record but also by the way you think it might be used in your paper. (The section marked "Kinds of Notecards," pp. 66 to 73, will indicate possible varieties.)

HOW TO TAKE NOTES

1. Write your notes on 4 × 6-inch index cards. You should always try to record the smallest practical piece of information on a card (you can always put two notecards together when you organize them, but it is difficult to separate one note into two). For that reason, you should write on one side of the card only and not continue the note onto a second card.

2. Before you take a single note from any source, take out the bibliography card that you have prepared for that source. Check each item of the bibliography card against the source in your hands to make sure that you have the complete and correct facts

concerning that particular source. Fill in any information you did not already have on the card.

Put a check mark on the bottom corner of the card to remind yourself that you have checked the accuracy of the bibliographical information directly from the book itself (and not from someone else's bibliography that may or may not be accurate).

Annotate your bibliography by making brief remarks on the back of the card. Make notes about whether the book has a chapter or just a few pages that will be useful to you, such as "chapter 3 (pp. 21 to 36) has genealogy and complete list of Egyptian gods. A time chart could be useful. Rest deals with history and not useful for me." Note also if the information is well documented from reliable sources, if it is gathered from original research, and if it has an extensive bibliography. Brief notes such as these will remind you later of what kind of information each book or article contains. You may not realize in your early note-taking stages that certain information would be useful, but later you might find that it would fit right into your argument, and you will save a lot of time by referring to your annotated bibliography cards to remind you of where you saw what.

3. Before you begin to take any notes, write the author's last name on the left corner of the top line. Leave the right side of the top line blank for a label (see STEP 6). If you use other books by the same author, you will need to differentiate among them by placing a comma and the title or a shortened form of it (Campbell, Inner). If you are using books by authors with the same last name, put the first name after the last (i.e., Smith, Henry and Smith, George).

4. Write only one idea from one source on each card. Make it a habit not to continue to a second card. Break the material into separate ideas. Never use a single card for notes from two sources. Notecards should be able to be organized in the order. determined by your outline later.

5. Put the page number in a circle before the first word on the note-card. If one idea is discussed on several pages in the source, indicate each page change by encircling the new page number before writing down the first word taken from that page. For

example: (36) "There are several factors . . .(37) The first factor . . . and (40) the second factor are important." Most Internet sources do not have page numbers so generally you will be unable to indicate where a piece of information is to be found within the document you are using. If, however, there are page numbers, paragraph or line numbers, or section numbers, be sure to use these on your notecard.

6. Early in your reading you will discover the need to adjust your reading speed to fit the material; not all printed material will be of equal value to you. When Bacon wrote that "some books are to be tasted, others to be swallowed, and some few to be chewed and digested," he could have been writing instructions to the student engaged in research. You must determine the relevance of each new source to your thesis and then decide how you will read it and what notes or information you need to take from it.

7. When you find the information that you want to use, decide what kind of note will suit your needs. Although some experienced researchers, particularly when they do not know exactly how they will use the information, prefer to take almost all notecards as direct quotes with plans to convert the information later into a paraphrase, summary, or other type of note, you may certainly use either paraphrase or summary. If you do take notes that are directly quoted, it is crucial that you use quotation marks on your card so that you will remember—even in the case of quoting just a few words—that the words within the quotation marks are not your own. It is essential to be accurate and concise in taking your notes in order to avoid the problem of plagiarism. (See "Plagiarism: A Step to Avoid" pp. 109 to 116.)

8. As you take your notes, you should enter the labels *in pencil* (since those labels may change) on the right-hand side of the top line of your notecard (see STEP 6). The label you enter will normally be one of the items (or a subpoint under it) from your preliminary outline.

9. Do not hesitate to take duplicating or contradictory notes; you may need them to defend your thesis later or to have a choice of sources to quote.

10. You do not need to document facts of common knowledge, such as "some people who have the AIDS virus are not aware that they have it." However, if you use a source that interprets or analyzes that fact, documentation is essential. Of course, your own analysis or interpretation or illustration of that fact need not be documented.

11. What you are reading may cause you to think of an idea that would relate to the material, or it may cause you to relate this material to something else you have read. It is both important and useful to record ideas like this on a notecard and to use them as you write your paper. One of your biggest contributions to the process, after all, is connecting pieces of information in ways that they have not been connected before in constructing an argument that is truly your own.

KINDS OF NOTECARDS

There are basically four kinds of notecards reflecting the different ways you can record information from a source: direct quotations, summaries, paraphrases, and your reactions to the information you are reading. This section will give you examples and discussions of each type. All the examples are taken from the Preface that is reproduced following the sample notecards at the end of STEP 5. That Preface is part of the master's thesis that is identified on the bibliography card reproduced on page 73.

A. Direct quotation. Be accurate; copy from the printed page exactly. Do not change the punctuation or the spelling; if there is an error, copy it and add sic in brackets to indicate that the error was found in the original. Enclose within double quotation marks all that you copy. (See card A1.)

Direct quotations are valuable especially if the impact of the material would be lost by summarizing or paraphrasing it or if the author has made his point in such a way that any other language would destroy or change its meaning. (See cards A1, A2a, and A2b.)

When there are double quotation marks within the passage you are copying, they will become single quotation marks within your double ones.

A1. The basic form; direct quotation of a complete passage:

A1

Markman

   "Later I realized that these
images are also found in
primitive art. Mitchell
explains that visual representation is 'not radically distinct from language,' and
Elizabeth Abel contends that
the underlying concepts of
myth and art are similar in
that both express a 'common
inner source whose subject
matter changes but whose
nature is the same.'"

**A2. Direct quotation of all or part of a passage with allow-
able changes:**

You may omit a portion within a quoted passage by using an
ellipsis (three periods with a space before and after each
period) when this portion is not relevant to your use of the
material. (See card A2a.)

A2a

Markman

   "But gradually I realized
that . . . those marvelous tales
were metaphorical expressions
of essential aspects of the
human condition."

You may add material of your own within a quoted passage
by enclosing it within brackets. (See card A2b.)

A2b

Markman

 "But gradually I realized
that on another level [other
than being fascinated by
the narratives and sense of
magic] those marvelous tales
were metaphorical expressions
of essential aspects of the
human condition."

In addition to the use of ellipsis and brackets to modify a quotation, you may:

- change capitalization to enable you to use the quotation as part of your own sentence,

- change punctuation when using a quotation within your own sentence to meet the requirements of your sentence,

- change verb tense to make the quoted material conform to your own sentence, or

- italicize to emphasize words not italicized in the original by adding, in parentheses, "italics mine" at the end of the passage, i.e., (italics mine). On a handwritten notecard you should indicate italics by underlining.

It is vital, however, that in making these minor changes, you do not alter the meaning of the quoted passage.

B. Summary. This kind of notecard states in your own words and condenses the basic ideas of a long passage, chapter, or even whole book.

B

Markman

 Verbal and visual expression serve similar functions with comparable imagery by which primitive societies have conceptualized their basic life experiences.

C. Paraphrase. This kind of notecard puts the information from the source into your own words. It differs from a summary, since the summary shortens the passage while a paraphrase is about the same length as the quoted passage. You should paraphrase when your wording would be more suitable for your paper than the wording of the source. You must be careful with this type of notecard to avoid using the words of the source without quotation marks, i.e., plagiarizing.

Use this with caution, for it is easy to be careless and end up being a plagiarist. You will avoid this danger if you read the passage well, close the book, and then write your paraphrase from memory. (See "Plagiarism: A Step to Avoid," pp. 109 to 116), and then check it for accuracy against the original.

C

Markman

 Markman states that the narratives and the magical aura of mythology are fascinating. In addition, one can read myths as a metaphoric expression of some important beliefs about life; they help a society to understand the mysteries of birth,

> death, and the relationship of
> man and nature. Even though
> these stories are not
> scientifically true, they do
> tell some basic truths about
> the human condition. Von Franz
> says that the imagery comes
> from the experience of every-
> day life or from the primor-
> dial images of man's psyche.
> Markman found that Mitchell
> and Abel documented her obser-
> vation that primitive art also
> serves this function and uti-
> lizes the same kinds of
> imagery. She thinks a compara-
> ble study of the verbal and
> visual arts of primitive soci-
> eties would be valuable. (P)

NOTE: Indicate the beginning of any paraphrase by informally men-
tioning the author and/or title, and be sure to note when other
authors need to be given credit for an idea, as with von Franz,
Mitchell, and Abel.

D. Reaction. You may wish to make an evaluation of the material
you are reading or to write down your own ideas about it. This
kind of note will remind you of judgments made during your
reading. Or the material you are reading may also cause you to
think of your own idea relating to it, or it may relate to ideas you
have read in other sources. Making a note of these reactions will
help you in organizing and writing your paper. You must make
clear on the card that the idea is not the author's if you give the
card the author's name. Often it is best not to write the author's
name at the top of the card, especially if your idea does not
relate only to that author; you might use "reaction" or simply
"me." (See card D.)

D

Markman

 Markman does not indicate clearly what the focus of the comparative study will be.

NOTE: Every completed notecard (see STEPS 6 and 7) should have five items on it:

1. source identification

2. page number in a circle

3. the note itself

4. quotation marks around direct quotes

5. the label or an outline symbol (see STEP 6)

PUNCTUATION WITH QUOTATION MARKS—REMEMBER THESE RULES:

All commas and periods go *inside* the closing quotation marks.

All other punctuation goes inside *only* when it is a part of the quoted matter.

PREFACE FROM WHICH NOTECARDS WERE TAKEN

The following reproduced Preface is the source for the sample note-cards given in the previous section. Note that it uses footnotes in Chicago style since there is no Works Cited page.

Preface

My earliest attraction to mythology was based on a
fascination with the dramatic action of the narratives and the aura of magic that pervades the world
in which that action takes place. But gradually I
realized that on another level those marvelous
tales were metaphorical expressions of essential
aspects of the human condition. Each social group
had obviously developed a mythology by which it
could understand the basic experiences of its existence, such as creation, nature, and death.
Although their mythological stories might not be
literally true, they do by analogy capture the
essential truth both of the society's world view
and of the basic nature of being. Von Franz says
that when man attempts to explain the unknown, he
is likely to depend on imagery from what he does
know or on archetypal images which come out of his
own inner experiences.[1] Later I realized that these
images are also found in primitive art. Mitchell
explains that visual representation is "not radically distinct from language,"[2] and Elizabeth Abel
contends that the underlying concepts of myth and
art are similar in that both express a "common
inner source whose subject matter changes but whose
nature is the same."[3] I was challenged to investigate the common denominators of the verbal and
visual expressions of these insights and to do a
comparative study of their metaphoric forms.

---

[1]Marie-Louise von Franz, *Patterns of Creativity
Mirrored in Creation Myths* (Zürich: Spring Publications, 1978), 5. Von Franz bases her conclusions on
the images she has found on maps of antiquity.

[2]W. J. T. Mitchell, "Spatial Form in Literature:
Toward a General Theory," *The Language of Images*,
ed. W. J. T. Mitchell (Chicago: University of
Chicago Press, 1980), 296. Mitchell reinforces his
point with a quote from Ludwig Wittgenstein's
Philosophical Investigations: "A picture held us

captive. And we could not get outside it, for it
lay in our language and language seemed to repeat
it to us inexorably." (271).

[3]Elizabeth Abel, "Redefining the Sister Arts:
Beaudelaire's Response to the Art of Delacroix,"
The Language of Images, ed. W. J. T. Mitchell
(Chicago: University of Chicago Press, 1980), 41.

BIBLIOGRAPHY CARD FOR PREFACE

Markman, Roberta H.
"The Metaphoric Vision in Mythology and Art."
Master's thesis,
California State University, Long Beach,
1994.

STEP

LABEL NOTECARDS
AND REVISE
WORKING OUTLINE

While you are taking your notes, you will see that they can be categorized under several general headings. Often these headings will coincide with the various units of your preliminary outline; on the other hand, they may suggest topics that need to be added to your outline. Remember, as you read, that you will not only be revising your preliminary outline but also reevaluating and reformulating your thesis statement in the light of your increased knowledge and accumulated information.

The items of your preliminary outline will provide the labels which you will write in pencil on the top lines of your notecards; pencil is better than ink here because you may want to change your label if you find later that a particular note could be used better under another heading. Some material cannot be categorized easily; leave these notecards to be labeled later. Some notes will be particularly good as part of an introduction or a conclusion; use "intro." or "concl." as the labels for these. Some notes will obviously not belong at all; mark these with an X and put them aside for the time being.

As you come closer to finishing your research, you will probably find that your notecards fall into three or four general categories, and these might turn out to be quite different from your original points for a temporary outline. You should now study your notecards and group them into these general categories. Simply separate your cards into stacks, according to the ideas on them. This may take considerable time, but it is time well spent for in this way you will determine the organization of your entire paper.

If, for example, you were writing a paper to compare the visual and verbal metaphors by which various cultures have attempted to understand the basic phenomena of life, you might see that your cards can easily be divided into the basic areas of life that are most frequently the concern of both mythology and art. These might include the expression of the process of creation, the relationship of the individual (microcosm) to the universal (macrocosm), the conception of death and an afterlife, and so forth. These classifications could then become the Roman numerals for your outline. Then you would further divide your cards into several subpoint labels, and one notecard might be labeled thus:

```
┌─────────────────────────────────────────────────────────────┐
│                                                               │
│  Markman          ˙    God related to life/death—also water  │
│  ─────────────────────────────────────────────────────────── │
│  ⟨27⟩    In many myths "Death is presented as a fig-         │
│          ure opposite, but complementary to, the             │
│          Creator as source of life." Sometimes a             │
│          twin who becomes God of the underworld.             │
│  ⟨28⟩    Water is also important to creation and yet         │
│          is often the means of destruction of the            │
│          world.                                               │
│                                                               │
└─────────────────────────────────────────────────────────────┘
```

NOTE: This card would go with III A 2 on the outline for the paper, page 102.

If, on the other hand, you were doing your research on the subject of smog control, you might find that your notecards would fall into such categories as causes of the smog problem, manifestations of the smog problem, effects of smog on various aspects of the environment, solutions to the problem of smog control. These general classifications would then supply the Roman numerals for your outline.

You may find other possibilities for different classifications by studying the following possible types of organization as they might relate to your subject. If you think you have sufficient information on only one aspect that is suggested, then select that narrower area for your paper and break that down further to create your outline.

problem—cause—effect—solution
social causes—political causes—economic causes—psychological causes

the various effects (or solutions or manifestations) of some problem

different kinds of irony or values or attitudes

different (or similar) characteristics of something or someone

different ways of evaluating your topic

different advantages (or disadvantages) of a particular method, machine, approach, or process

Comparing and contrasting is a particularly instructive and creative way of organizing a documented paper. It enables the student to come to valuable conclusions by "measuring" one idea or area in terms of another. There are, however, three basic considerations to keep in mind:

1. Be sure before you begin that the two areas to be compared and contrasted have just enough in common to make them comparable without being ridiculously obvious or impossibly unrelated.

2. Be sure to qualify your points by telling to what extent and how one area is different from the other, thus avoiding the risk of overstating your case to the point of losing its credibility.

3. Be sure to compare and contrast the two areas *point by point* rather than discussing *all* of one area and then *all* of the other, thereby forcing your readers to determine the similarities and differences for themselves.

4. Be sure to cover the same points for both areas.

REVISING YOUR OUTLINE

(See also TEMPORARY OUTLINE, STEP 3, pp. 12 to 13 and STEP 7, #2 on pp. 79 to 82.)

After you have found a way to divide your notecards into separate larger classifications, mark with a Roman numeral I all the cards in the classification you think you will discuss first in your paper; use a II for those you will discuss in the second part, and so on. Then take all the ones you have marked with numeral I and, considering them as you would material for a separate essay, determine into what categories you can further divide those ideas. For example, you might find that the pile of cards marked I, because they all deal with the causes of the smog problem, contain some that deal with problems related to industry, others deal with problems related to transportation, others with problems related to private homes. These would be divided into IA, IB, and IC. Then you would consider each of these sections separately. You might decide that those cards marked IA or IB do not need further division, but that those marked IC need to be divided into such categories as road transportation and air transportation, and you would mark the cards appropriately IC 1 and IC 2.

Remember in your outlining that you can never have a I without at least a II, nor an A without at least a B, nor a 1 without at least a 2, since logically nothing can be divided into fewer than two parts (not even apples.) And your outline actually represents a division of ideas for the purpose of analyzing a subject in an organized fashion. At first, then, your notecards might have a label like the preceding example; but once your outline is really set, you can save time by simply using the outline number instead.

Now you are ready to write the outline in its final form, taking care to word the items so that all Roman numerals (subdivisions of your thesis) are worded to be parallel in logic and in grammar; all the letter entries (A, B, C) are stated as parallel subdivisions of the Roman numeral under which they appear; and all the numbered entries (1, 2, 3) are logically and grammatically parallel subdivisions of the statement made in the letter under which they appear.

Before you can decide that you have finished your note-taking, you should examine your notecards and your revised outline to determine if you have adequate material for all the areas that are important to your thesis or a particular part of its proof. This evaluation will direct any subsequent note-taking to those specific topics for which you need more information, and you will then take only those notes that you know you will use. If you do take more notes on some new material that necessitates the inclusion of a new point, be sure to change your outline to include it.

ERRORS FREQUENTLY FOUND IN STUDENT OUTLINES

There are two major problems often made in constructing the outline that will result in problems with the paper itself:

1. The thesis is too broad and cannot be adequately supported in the space limitation of the paper. See STEP 3.

2. The major points do not relate directly to the thesis, and the sub-points do not "break down" the major point above it. Consequently, there will be material in the final paper that does not relate to the thesis. Just because you have some information on a notecard does not mean it will be relevant to your point.

STEP

WRITE THE FIRST DRAFT

Although you will never have the feeling that you have finished your note-taking to your satisfaction and you will never lose the feeling that you could do a much better job if you could examine "just one more source," the time for writing the first draft inevitably comes.

1. Check your thesis; be sure that it states as specifically as possible in a simple declarative sentence exactly what the material you have gathered adds up to.

2. Check your outline; be sure that each subtopic is directly relevant to the more general topic above it and, finally, that each major topic is directly relevant to the thesis. Make each item parallel to every other item both logically and grammatically. (That is, in a sentence outline, which is definitely preferable to a topic outline, be sure that each item is stated in a full sentence; in a topic outline, be sure that all terms are stated in parallel parts of speech, which are also parallel logically.) Check to see that no item overlaps another. Remember that no item can be divided into just one part: every I must have a II, every A must have a B, every 1 must have a 2, and so forth. Check to see that you have arranged the items of your outline in logical order: order of space or time, order of importance, order of complexity, and so forth. REMEMBER: Just as it is better and more advantageous to detect the faults in a floor plan for a house on the blueprint

than it is to find them in the finished building, so it is easier and more advantageous to find the errors of your logic and organization in your outline than it is to find them in your finished paper.

3. Your outline should now be ready for you to write in its final form if you have followed the instructions in STEP 6. (See sample outline STEP 10 pp. 101 to 102.) If you have some notecards you cannot use (there are inevitably a few), put them away, for you may be able to use them in writing some other paper in the future.

4. Do not begin by writing your introduction. Wait to write that when your paper is completed and you can see what you are introducing. Start now by putting on paper as quickly as possible the overall information you wish to convey about your major points and their subdivisions. Save the fun of polishing your style until later; first you must capture your ideas on paper so you can think about them.

   Develop your first point first. Arrange the notecards for your first Roman numeral to correspond with the order in that part of your outline and plunge right in as if you were writing a short essay with Roman numeral I as your thesis.

5. The complete thesis of the section should appear early in the section so that your reader knows where you are going. Topic sentences (usually a point on your outline) generally come at the beginning of paragraphs and then they are developed by giving examples, descriptions, and facts and figures taken from your research. Be sure that all the quoted or paraphrased material is carefully analyzed so that the reader knows how and why you are using that particular material to make your point.

6. If you are not using a computer, write on one side of the paper only and skip a line between each line of your writing so that you can cross out poor or awkward phrases and add better wording without unnecessary recopying later when you revise. If you are using a computer, you can move the material around very easily, of course.

7. Try to use direct quotations very sparingly in your paper. Use them only when there is no other way the material can be stated and when the exact words of the author must be used to make your point. Copy the quotations very carefully, using identical punctuation and wording of the original. If you are writing on a computer, you may simply "paste" the quotations in.

It is very important to learn how to "weave" quoted or paraphrased material so that it becomes a part of your own text. Try not to use the colon to introduce any quotation unless it is long enough to block (i.e., one over three lines in length); otherwise, weave quotations into your own sentences so that a person hearing the paper read aloud would be unable to tell where a quote actually begins or ends. Make all quoted material sound like an integral part of your whole work; this means you must pay attention to point of view and tense, and provide necessary lead-ins and transitions to the material. Not only does integrating the source material into your text add to the general unity and fluency of your writing, it also serves the even more important purpose of indicating the relevance of that source material to the content of your paper. In other words, before using a quoted or paraphrased passage, think of why you are using it or of what purpose it serves in your paragraph; then weave it into your text by indicating some relevance, which you clarify in your own wording. It will then be valuable to your proof of thesis, and its implications will be clear to your reader.

For example, in the following sentence from a discussion of Gerhart Hauptmann's play *The Weavers*, there is no doubt about the significance of the quotation used:

> The formula for success, which according to Master Wiegand is "cunning, quickness, and ruthless determination" (30), had to be exposed and challenged.

Poorly used, the quotation might be inserted without any indication of relevance to the purpose of the paper, which (as here) might be a study of the values questioned in the play. An example of the same quotation, ineptly used, might read thus:

> Master Wiegand said: "Cunning, quickness, and ruthless determination are necessary" (30).

Your reader would naturally wonder, "Necessary for what?" You might profit at this point by studying the sample paper on pages 103 to 108, which illustrates a variety of ways to incorporate quotations into your text. Note the punctuation also.

As you are writing, check carefully to see whether

a. you are not merely "stringing quotations" together without enough of your own wording;

b. you have already put a check mark on the notecard to show that you have previously used that material;

c. you have introduced each quoted passage with an appropriate transition;

d. you have analyzed your source material to make it work for you in your paper by showing your reader specifically how it applies to your argument. Don't just cite a quotation and rush on. You have just stated that someone said something; now answer the question, "So what?" Why are you telling this to your reader?

8. Even before you finish the first writing (rough draft), you may want to rearrange some material already written. If so, see the first paragraph under STEP 8; the directions there will facilitate your work if you decide to insert or change material as you write.

9. When you have taken information from a notecard, whether it is a directly quoted passage or not, stop where the passage ends. Insert the author and page number taken from your notecard, in parentheses, here. It is essential to copy this information exactly. It is the only way that you can be assured that your documentation is accurate.

If you are using a computer, you may have a program that will insert the footnotes for you at the bottom of the page, but note that MLA does not use footnotes for citations. See "Using Footnotes or Endnotes" and "Procedure for Writing Footnotes or Endnotes" and "Footnote or Endnote Forms" in Appendix B. Put a check mark in the bottom left corner of a notecard once you have used the information on it so that you will be sure not to use the same material again.

10. Develop each section of your outline considering each as a separate essay for the time being. Just as you could not expect to write five essays in one day, so you cannot hope to develop more than one section of a long paper at a time.

11. Remember to revise your outline if you make any changes as you write your first draft. By the time you complete your first draft your outline will be the blueprint of your actual paper.

12. Be sure to number pages of your first draft or have the computer do it for you automatically.

CHECK LIST FOR FREQUENT ERRORS IN WRITING THE RESEARCH PAPER

When you have finished your first draft, it is important to look over your writing, checking particularly for basic errors that frequently appear on the final draft. It is a good idea for you to find them yourself before handing in a paper; if you don't, your instructor will. Of course all the rules of good writing—including grammatical structure, coherence, unity, good paragraphing, correct spelling, and accurate choice of words—apply, but the items on the list of problems that follows are frequently corrected on student research papers:

1. your sources are not integrated. You use all material from one source and then all from another; your reader could just pick up one book and read certain pages and then the next one. Real research involves the blending together of ideas from many different sources. (See p. 86.)

2. using phrases that are too similar to the words of your source and that would be considered plagiarized. (See pp. 109 to 119.)

3. not giving the source of an item of information; all information from sources *must* be documented. (See pp. 89 to 90 and 109 to 119.)

4. using incorrect bibliographical form. (See pp. 29 to 53.)

5. using obsolete publications for a current subject such as computer technology, treatments for disease, or cultural phenomena that change quickly and radically.

6. using sources that are not reliable and whose information is not documented. (See p. 15.)

7. using a quotation without analyzing, thus leaving it up to the reader to decide how it fits into your argument. (See p. 81.)

8. moving from one idea to another without transitions that indicate to the reader what the relationship is between the two ideas. Use transitional phrases such as "as a result," "consequently," "on the other hand," and "another less important reason." (See pp. 81 and 85.)

9. overusing the passive voice, i.e., "it was decided that such and such was true" should be changed to "Professor Jones decided that such and such was true."

STEP

REVISE THE TEXT;
WRITE INTRODUCTION
AND CONCLUSION

The best way to revise your work is to begin by reading your paper aloud after a waiting period. Does it sound clear? Do the paragraphs seem clearly connected? Do you guide the reader through the paper by providing transitions and repeating key terms? By reading it aloud you will be able to identify problems that you can correct. If a portion of your paper should be moved, you can accomplish that with your computer's cut and paste function. Or, if you are not using a computer, you can simply use scissors to cut the portion that belongs elsewhere and tape (or "paste") it where it should go. This method of revision, dating to when people still used paste, was the origin of the "cut" and "paste" commands on your computer. It is essential that you keep the footnote or parenthetical reference with the material it documents. Accuracy in this regard is crucial. Computer bibliographical programs will do this for you when you move text, but be very careful if you are moving text on your own.

As you work through your draft:

1. Check to see that you have followed the basic rules for sentence structure and style.

2. Check to see that you have followed the principles of rhetoric in organization, paragraph development, and diction.

3. Check to see that you have smooth transitions (connections) from sentence to sentence, paragraph to paragraph, and section to section. Check particularly to see that the quoted material is integrated into the text so that, together with your writing, it presents a unified piece of work. When you hear a well-prepared lecture, you are not aware that the lecturer has gathered material from many different sources, part of which he or she is quoting directly and some of which is being paraphrased. You should give the same impression to your reader. Often the addition of a few connecting words will result in smooth transitions.

4. Check to see that your finished paper sounds logically developed and that everything that you have included in your paper presents relevant, logical proof of your thesis. Draw a line through anything that does not, and eliminate it now.

5. Check to see that you have avoided the repetition of facts or ideas. A "padded" paper is boring and meaningless.

6. Be sure that specific examples are provided for all general statements whether they are from other sources or your own. Most ideas need to be explained and/or illustrated in order to be clear.

WRITE THE INTRODUCTION

Now that you know exactly what you are about to introduce, you can write an introductory section to your paper. You can use your introduction to do the following:

1. point out the timeliness or value of your research;

2. define an abstract or special term used in your thesis;

3. explain why you have taken this particular aspect of your topic;

4. inform your reader of the various aspects of your topic other than the one you have chosen;

5. give a pertinent anecdote that provides a direct means of leading into your topic;

6. summarize how you have approached your topic.

Whatever your approach, your introduction should be relevant; it should gain the immediate attention of your reader, and it should clarify your thesis in some way.

WRITE THE CONCLUSION

The conclusion of the research paper is the most valuable single part of it. All the material you have gathered means nothing to your reader until you present the conclusion you have reached as a result of your research. Restate your thesis and show what the material you have presented adds up to. Analyze and evaluate your main points for your reader; also consider the ramifications and general implications of them to your conclusion. Although no actual new information is usually introduced in the concluding paragraphs, the conclusion is the primary "original" contribution you offer in your paper. It manifests the value of your research as well as your understanding of the material that you have presented. It should be a strong recapitulation of your major ideas.

Now read the entire paper aloud again and listen to how it sounds. It should flow smoothly throughout; supply transitions wherever you sense a lack of continuity from one idea to the next.

STEP

COMPLETE AND CHECK PARENTHETICAL REFERENCES ON DRAFT

All information taken from the work of others needs to be documented. Normally, every paragraph except those that develop your own completely original ideas will have at least one parenthetical reference or footnote.

WHAT TO DOCUMENT

All important statements of fact and all opinions, whether directly quoted or paraphrased, and all paraphrases of those facts that are not common knowledge should be documented by a footnote or parenthetical reference to the exact page in the source where you found your information. If you are not quoting printed matter, your parenthetical reference or footnote should tell the reader where and how you found out the particular material you need to document.

WHAT NOT TO DOCUMENT

1. Well-known, generally accepted facts need not be documented unless you want to document someone's questioning or analysis of those facts.

2. Any material that comes from commonly recognized sources or quotations need not be documented; you may say that all men are created equal or that all the world's a stage or that the heavens declare the glory of God without referring in context or footnote to the Declaration of Independence, to Shakespeare, or to the Bible, respectively.

STYLES OF DOCUMENTATION

In the past, citations documenting the sources of the material in the paper were placed at the bottom of each page (footnotes) or gathered together at the end of the paper (endnotes) with corresponding numbers in the text. The "Preface" reproduced on pp. 72 and 73 illustrates this practice. Current MLA form, as well as most other forms currently used, has replaced this method of documentation with one using parenthetical references within the text itself. This is probably the form of documentation you will use, and it is the one we will present in the sample paper. In this system footnotes are only used for:

1. Definitions that would interrupt the text but might be helpful to the reader. (See footnote 3 of Sample Paper 1 (p. 108) and footnote 27 of Sample Paper 2 (p. 145).)

2. Material that would detract from the focus of your paper but that would supply valuable and enriching information to the reader. This material may be in your own words or in words you quote from an authority. Also, the footnote may simply refer the reader to another source or sources where a fuller discussion may be found. (See footnotes 1 and 5 of Sample Paper 1 (p. 108) and footnotes 5 and 36 of Sample Paper 2 (pp. 143 and 145).)

3. Cross-references to other parts of your own paper. (See footnote 4 of Sample Paper 1 (p. 108) and footnote 29 of Sample Paper 2 (p. 145).)

USING PARENTHETICAL REFERENCES

Parenthetical references are much simpler than footnotes or endnotes. These references basically provide the author's last name and a page number to identify the source and the specific location within it from which your material came. Further information regarding the source can be found in the Works Cited page of your paper. Therefore the information in the parenthetical reference must match the corresponding information in the Works Cited. Sample Paper 1 (pp. 103 to 108) is documented in this fashion.

Since you have used parenthetical references in writing the draft of your paper, most of the work of this form of documentation has already been done. Now you should check to make sure that it has been done properly and accurately. The following guidelines will help you do this:

1. Place the reference as close as possible to the material it documents, but only where a pause would naturally occur, such as at the end of a sentence. The parenthetical documentation precedes the punctuation mark that concludes the sentence, clause, or phrase containing the material you have used. If the quotation comes at the end of the sentence, the parenthetical reference should be placed after the closing quotation mark and before the concluding punctuation mark.

2. Within the parentheses there is no punctuation between the author's name and the page number. The abbreviation for page is never used, and there is never any end punctuation within the parentheses.

3. Take out the bibliography card to make sure that you have copied the author's name exactly. Make a check mark on the card to remind yourself that you have used that source and that it must be included in your final Works Cited.

FORMS FOR PARENTHETICAL REFERENCES

1. If the work to be cited was written by a single author and is alphabetized in the bibliography under the author's last name, your parenthetical reference will give the author's last name followed

by a page number: (Jay 26). In the case of an Internet source that does not have page numbers, you would give the author's name only in the parentheses.

2. If you have already given the author's name in your text in connection with this material, then you would give only the page number in the reference: (37). In the case of an Internet source that does not have page numbers, you would give the author's name in the text, and there would be no parentheses. In the case of multiple authors of a single work or a corporate author with a long name, it is preferable to mention the name or names in the text, leaving just the page number for the parenthetical reference, rather than having a long, unwieldy parenthetical reference that would interrupt the flow of your writing.

3. If there is no author, that is, if your bibliographical entry begins with a title, use the title or the first word under which it is alphabetized if it is long: (*Máscaras* 26).

4. If there are two authors, use both last names: (Markman and Markman 123). If there are three, use all three (Broda, Carrasco, and Matos Moctezuma ix). If there are more than three, use the first author's last name followed by "and others": (Lothrop and others 87).

5. If there is no author, but the Works Cited entry begins with the name of an editor, a translator, or a compiler, use the last name of that person followed by the page number: (Apostolos-Cappadona 86).

6. If the author is a corporate entity, or if the work cited is a government document, use the name of the originating entity or the first word under which it is alphabetized: (Instituto Guerrerense de la Cultura 21) or (Instituto 21).

7. If your reference is to one volume in a multi-volume set, give the author's last name followed by the volume number, a colon, and the page number: (Budge 2:23).

In the case of nonprint media (records, films, television and radio shows, etc.) there will, of course, be no page number: (Brahms).

8. If the bibliography contains only one work by the author cited, you should give only the author's last name to identify the work

unless, of course, there were two authors with the same last name in which case you would have to give the first name too.

9. If there is more than one book by the author in the bibliography, give the title or an abbreviated form of it after the author's name: (Campbell. *Inner Reaches* 86).

10. Remember that the point of your documentation is to direct the reader to the correct source in your Works Cited where the rest of the information can be found and to give the precise page, volume of a multivolume work, or act, scene, and line of a play from which the material came in that source. References should be kept as brief as possible as long as the accuracy of locating the material is assured.

    Footnotes should still be used for material that would disrupt the flow of the text, such as definitions, explanations, and cross-references. (See items 1, 2, and 3, p. 90.) Also if you need to refer to several sources, it is best to cite them in a footnote.

STEP

PUT THE PAPER IN FINAL FORM

THE ELEMENTS

1. Format

Probably your instructor will give you specific instructions regarding the format of your final paper. If not, you may follow these suggestions. A research paper should be typed or printed on regular paper and double-spaced. Leave good margins on all four sides of the paper, allowing sufficient extra room on the left side for binding. The finished paper may begin with a title page.

2. Title Page

The title page, if there is one, is a page on which you state the title of the paper, your name, the course (and section number, if any) for which the paper was written, the name of the institution (often considered optional), and the date the paper is submitted.

The MLA Handbook does not call for a title page. Rather, "beginning one inch from the top of the first page and flush with the left margin, type your name, your instructor's name, the course number, and the date on separate lines, double-spacing between the lines. Double-space again and center the title." Then double-space once more and begin your paper (116).

3. Dedication Page or Preface

The dedication page or the preface, if there is one, is inserted after the title page; it is not numbered. The title of the page, "Dedication" or "Preface," is centered. If you do not have a title page, you would not have a "Dedication" or "Preface."

4. Outline

The outline page, if there is one, serves as a table of contents, although it is not necessary to show page numbers for a short paper. The title of the page, "Outline," is centered. The page is numbered, and since the first page of your outline is headed by a title, the number is centered at the bottom of the page. The number is given in Roman numerals (lowercase) because nothing is numbered in Arabic numerals until the first page of the text.

After the title, "Outline," skip two lines and state the thesis sentence (after the word Thesis:). Follow that statement with the outline proper.

5. First Page of Text

The title of your paper is centered on the first (and no other) page of the text.

6. Documentation

The parenthetical references will be written exactly as they are on the rough draft of your paper. For detailed information concerning documentation on the final copy, see STEP 9.

7. Pagination

Every page that is headed by a title is numbered at the bottom center of that page. The number is written usually without punctuation. The pages are numbered consecutively from the first. All other pages of the paper are numbered in the upper right-hand corner of the page. The pages are numbered consecutively from the first page of the text to the last page of the bibliography. All pages, such as those of the outline, if there is one, preceding the first page of the text of the paper are numbered with lowercase Roman numerals; the text and everything following it is numbered with Arabic numerals.

8. Quotations

Short quotations: Quoted short passages and/or sentences are woven into the text of your paragraph and should blend smoothly with your own style and the tense you are using. In the sample research paper on pages 103 to 108, you will see many examples of quotations (and paraphrases) woven into the text and made meaningful by the context in which they appear. Notice that before and after each quoted passage the punctuation is determined by what is needed to make the passage fit smoothly into the sentence. In other words, the test for punctuating before or after a quoted passage is this: Would you need a mark of punctuation at that point in your sentence if there were no quotation marks?

Longer (blocked) quotations: Sometimes, a quoted passage is too long to be woven into your own sentence; it is an entity in itself and must be set off from the paragraph in which it appears. In fact, any directly quoted material that is longer than four lines must be "blocked," i.e., its left margin is indented from the left margin of the paper. No quotation marks are needed, since this "blocking" indicates it is a quotation. To indicate a quotation within this quotation, use double quotation marks. If there is a paragraph indentation in the original, you may indicate that with a further indentation. See the Sample Paper, p. 106, for an example.

9. Works Cited

The Works Cited is always the last section of a research paper. (See STEP 4 for final Works Cited forms.)

10. Final Step

Proofread your paper carefully for typographical errors.

A SAMPLE RESEARCH PAPER

The sample research paper reproduced here is documented using MLA parenthetical reference form. For a sample paper using Chicago style endnotes and bibliography, see the Appendix (pp. 138 to 149).

NOTE: Since it is neither expedient nor necessary to reproduce an entire paper for the sake of illustrating the techniques explained in this manual, the pages that follow contain a full sentence outline and only that part of the paper that expands the thesis. (Normally, the first part of any research paper, the introduction, develops the thesis and clarifies the point of view from which the writer has limited his or her paper.) Also included is a bibliography listing only the sources used in this introductory section of the longer paper by Markman, from which this introductory section is taken. Normally, a short research paper such as this one would not have as many footnotes or as much quoted material; however, it is important for the student to see how a wide variety of material could be used and documented.

Words and Pictures:
The Mythic Vision in Tales and Art

by

Roberta H. Markman

Comparative Literature 452, Section I
California State University, Long Beach
January 3, 1994

Outline

Thesis: Humanity's attempt to understand the basic
phenomena of life is expressed metaphorically both verbally in mythology and visually in mythic art.

I. The process of creation is expressed
metaphorically in both mythology and
art.

A. Both mythology and art express the
concept of genesis through the
metaphoric image of the joining of
opposites.

1. Sometimes the primordial couple
(the joining of masculine and
feminine) provides the metaphor
in both mythology and art.

2. Sometimes the integration of
light and dark is the metaphoric
image for the creative process
in both mythology and art.

3. Sometimes the weaving of warp
and woof (vertical and horizon-
tal) serves as the imagery for
creation.

B. Both mythology and art express the
concept of creation through the
metaphor of the sun's pattern of
dying and rising.

C. Both mythology and art show "the
beginning" through the imagery of
order emerging from chaos.

D. Both mythology and art express the
creative process as the splitting
of the whole, or single image, into
two or more of its parts.

i

II. Humanity's relationship to the universe is expressed metaphorically in both mythology and art.

A. Both mythology and art describe various aspects of nature in their relationship to the individual to show the complex relationship of the individual to the universal.

B. Both mythology and art use the imagery of the human being and God(s) to express and understand the relationship of the unique to the general.

III. The conception of death and an afterlife are metaphorically expressed in both mythology and art in an attempt to come to terms with these mysteries.

A. The phenomenon of a symbolic death is expressed metaphorically in both mythology and art.

1. The imagery of humanity's transcendent temporal experience is expressed metaphorically in both mythology and art.

2. The imagery of the human being's return from death, darkness, or the underworld to a new life is often the metaphor for the experience of death and resurrection.

B. Physical death and a spiritual return, or transcendence, is shown metaphorically in both mythology and art.

SAMPLE PAPER USING PARENTHETICAL REFERENCE STYLE

Note that endnotes are used within a paper using the parenthetical reference style to present information other than the reference. The endnotes included here represent a range of possibilities: an explanatory endnote (#1), the reference for a quotation documented in the work cited (#2), a definition (#3), a cross-reference to your own paper (#4), and the notation of an additional source of information confirming, contradicting, or amplifying the source cited (#5).

Words and Pictures:
The Mythic Vision in Tales and Art

Human beings everywhere have always been curious. They look around their world, poke and pry into its features, in order to understand everything that confronts them. We can see evidence of this even in the oldest stories that have come down to us. In the epic of *Gilgamesh*, from the second or third millennium B.C., for example, as in the later story of creation in Genesis, people were challenged to "name" the animals and the other features of their world. This "naming" is significant on many levels, but in its most symbolic sense it signifies their coming to understand the basic nature of things. In fact, the Biblical account of creation makes clear that the development of that understanding is God's intention in setting the task of naming (Genesis 1:26 and 2:19) and that the understanding involves an awareness of the relationship of what they have "named" to the "final, indivisible presence of Being itself" (Gingerich 109), that is, to God, thereby understanding it in the most fundamental sense.

As this suggests, human beings have always known that the world they inhabit consists of more than observable reality, and their curiosity has always extended beyond what they could see or touch. The same early stories show us that such aspects of life as creation and death, aspects that exist beyond the realms of intellect and logic, were similarly named and thus understood. This "naming," however, has not always been verbal; the same need to understand is the most powerful impetus for the creation of visual art in traditional societies (Wingert 30), for such mythic art serves "to kindle into meaning [for human beings] aspects of their perception that would otherwise remain external to their minds" (Taylor 31). The ability to "name" what had been unknown provides the psychological security that human beings have always sought.

The curious individual, whether of one of today's technologically sophisticated, urban societies or of a "primal"[1] society of the present or distant past, begins this search for understanding with a question, and that question triggers the search that leads ultimately to an understanding that can be communicated through the fashioning of a mythic story or image (Eliade, *Images* 55-56). This is necessarily a process that begins in the individual since "the myths are metaphorical of spiritual potentiality in the [individual] human being, and the same powers that animate our life animate the life of the world" (Campbell, *Power* 22). The mythic images created as a result of the search express metaphorically the understanding that has been achieved, an understanding of the realm beyond the observable. Since myths and art use metaphors in that way to "speak about the unknowable in terms of the known" (Sproul 11), they are able to transmit the understanding of reality that results from the creative response to a confrontation with the unknown (Waardenburg 64).

Because they answer humanity's seemingly universal basic questions in particular ways, the myths define the cultures that create them (Watts xi), and, conversely, they serve an important educational function in their community by expressing "the wisdom of life" as understood by that culture (Campbell *Power* 55). Pemberton illustrates this point in his discussion of the verses of the *Odu* recited by Ifa diviners of the African Yoruba culture. Through them he demonstrates that myth and art, by expressing the world view and values of their particular culture, explain the

varying roles of human beings and the powers that
shape their lives as well as help the Yoruba society
understand how to cope with its problems (66).
Because myths serve such functions as these, there
seems to be no question among scholars that myth is
essential to existence (Freund 233) or that "mere
purposive rationality," on the other hand, "unaided
by such phenomena as art, religion, dream . . . is necessarily pathogenic and destructive of life."[2]

Thus both mythology and mythic art create a kind
of cosmic order out of what appears to be chaos
(Segy 8), and by so doing are clearly not the opposite of science (Sproul 16) or less valuable than
logic (Bolle 5). "Myths are fictional, to be sure,
but that fictional need not mean unreal and certainly
not unempirical" (Doty 4). The great myths, like
great art, are concerned with capturing the essence
of their subjects. Dorothy Jean Ray points this out
in her discussion of an Eskimo mask when she
explains how the image on the mask captures not an
individual animal, "but the vital force representing
a chain or continuum of all the individual spirits
of that genus which had lived, were living, or were
to live" (10). Its "truth," then, is not dependent
on reproducing the details of a particular visual
reality. Going "beyond" the object in that way permits a freedom from the limitations of the " 'historic moment' " (Eliade, *Images* 13). It is in this
sense that "the artist penetrates—at times dangerously—into the depths of the world and his own psyche" (Eliade "The Sacred" 83), and it is for this
reason and in this way that "the artist . . . brings
the images of a mythology to manifestation; without
images (whether mental or visual) there is no mythology" (Campbell, *Inner* 19).

These images may be expressed either in words or
graphically, and scholars have compared the verbally
expressed mythology and the visually expressed mythic
art of primal societies by considering their methodologies as well as their functions and thematic concerns. Human beings think in images and, according to
von Franz, "the only reality we can talk about . . . is

the *image* of reality in our field of consciousness"
(11). Thus Jacques Waardenburg can say that a myth
"can be called a 'moving symbolism'" (54). Others
have also investigated this relationship. Cassirer
points out that "word magic is everywhere accompanied by picture magic" (98), and Abel shows that
both narrative myths and mythic art express a "common inner source whose subject matter changes but
whose nature is the same" (41).

Ultimately, however, there is no doubt that

> the relationship between word and image is,
> potentially, at once metonymic[3] and meta-
> phoric: metonymic in that the two complete
> each other sequentially and as parts of a
> whole: metaphoric in that each translates
> into the other's medium. Ideally, image
> melts into speech, speech crystallizes the
> immediacy of the image (Gilman 63).

Thus it is primarily as metaphors that art and
mythology are able to serve as "poetic expressions of
. . . transcendental seeing."[4] By bringing together
"*two frames of reference* of which the reader [or
viewer] must be simultaneously aware" (Barbour 13),
both art and mythology "bring truth into being" (Segy
10) and serve the essential functions that have been
attributed to them. By juxtaposing everyday experiences to the images of imagination, the mundane is
metaphorically transformed into a revelation of the
"'extraordinary' aspects of ordinary reality" (Waardenburg 43-44). As he wears a mask or plays out his
mythology in a ritual, "the man of the archaic societies becomes conscious of himself in an 'open world'
that is rich in meaning" (Eliade, *Images* 178),
detaching himself from his narrow environment (Foss
146). It follows, then, that "'to live' a symbol [in
ritual] and to decipher the messages [of ritual and
myth] correctly is equivalent to gaining access to
the universal" (Eliade, "The Symbolism" 13).

For traditional societies if the images created by
the visual and verbal arts are not "the vessels of

spiritual revelation," they fail as art and become mere "things."[5] It is the very nature and power of the metaphor that keep art and mythology from becoming "things." By creating and maintaining the tension between the known and the unknown, the conscious and the unconscious, the outer and the inner, the past and the present, "the metaphor has the task of destroying the rigid reduction and limitations of the word" (Foss 120) and of bringing two images together in a process that remains "eternally alive and universally accessible" (Eliade, *Images* 173); yet it must, as David Attenborough says of a Dogon sculpture, "be understood in its own terms" (140), as it would have been by its creator. In myth "the word [or image] speaks as if vested with its own authority" (Veyne 110), for "myths convey what a culture has chosen as its most important symbolic interpretations" (Doty 117).

Clearly then, "images, symbols and myths are not irresponsible creations of the psyche; they respond to a need and fulfill a function, that of bringing to light the most hidden modalities of being" (Eliade, *Images* 12). "Reaching into depths into which our daily life with its various rituals can scarcely follow" (Foss 110), they capture the essence of the human condition and force us to realize that the human race cannot be divided into "primitives" and moderns; there is a unity in the structure of humanity, and no one group can be considered inferior to another (Bolle xiii). "The needs, aspirations, and longings of mankind are similar" (Wingert 72), and as we investigate the various manifestations of the human attempt to understand the basic phenomena of life through the metaphorical expression of insights, both visually in art and verbally in mythology, we will find that they speak to all people in "a language of vision which may tell us things about ourselves . . . that words alone cannot touch" (Mitchell 298-299). They will fulfill what Joseph Campbell calls "the most essential service of a mythology," that "of opening the mind and heart to the utter wonder of all being" (*Inner* 18).

ENDNOTES

[1]Following Jamake Highwater's suggestion (xix), I will use *primal* instead of *primitive* when discussing technologically undeveloped traditional cultures to avoid the negative connotations of the latter term.

[2]Gregory Bateson, *Steps to an Ecology of Mind*; quoted in Bob Samples, ix.

[3]metonymic: using the name of one thing for that of another of which it is an attribute or with which it is associated.

[4]Campbell, *Myths* 31; specific illustrations of various metaphoric images and an explicit discussion of the ability of metaphor to transcend the mundane and profane by creatively expressing insights into the basic phenomena of life will be developed in the body of this paper; see outline on pages i-ii.

[5]Foss 111; see also *Máscaras* 15: "en muchas ocasiones la elaboracion de la mascara es parte del ritual y requiere que el individual este en un estado de pureza fisica y espiritual."

PLAGIARISM: A STEP TO AVOID*

The only problem of composition that is unique to the research paper is this: you must use and work with the ideas and words of other scholars. Before you are ready for this privilege and its attendant responsibility, you must understand and remember that an idea, though not a tangible article, is just as much the property of another as that person's car or clothes; often it is much more valuable. You must not use it without properly acknowledging your indebtedness. This acknowledgment, far from weakening your paper, will in fact add value and authority to your writing.

If every student understood clearly what plagiarism is, the following illustrations would not be necessary. However, the question of what is honest and what is dishonest use of source material is one that plagues many students; many of the unwary and uninformed have suffered serious consequences academically. As with the entire philosophical question of honesty, there are various degrees of plagiarism. If these examples and your own conscience are inadequate guides, consult the person who is guiding your work on your research paper.

---

*The illustrations for this section are based on the preface reproduced on pages 72 to 73. It is also reproduced as part of the explanation for the paraphrases (pages 113 to 116) at the end of this section on plagiarism.

WORD-FOR-WORD PLAGIARISM

I was attracted to mythology because of my fascination with the dramatic action of the stories and the feeling of magic that enters the world in which that action happens. But gradually I realized that on another level those marvelous tales were metaphorical expressions of essential aspects of the human condition. Each social group had obviously developed a body of myths by which it could understand the basic experiences of its existence, such as creation, death, and nature. Although these mythological stories might not be literally true, they do by analogy capture the essential truth both of the basic nature of being and of the society's world view. Von Franz says that when people attempt to explain the unknown, they are likely to depend on imagery from what they do know or on archetypal images which come out of their own inner experiences. Later I realized that these images are also found in primitive art. Mitchell explains that visual representation is not radically distinct from language, and Elizabeth Abel claims that the underlying concepts of myth and art are similar in that both express a common inner source in which the subject matter changes but the nature is the same. I was challenged to investigate the common denominators of the verbal and visual expressions of these insights and to do a comparative study of their metaphoric forms.

COMMENT: Transposing or substituting a few words will not create a paraphrase. In this example, after saying "I was attracted to" instead of "My earliest attraction," the writer of this nearly verbatim piece of plagiarism simply used different words or reworded some short phrases: "was based on" was changed to "because of my"; "narratives" became "stories"; "pervades" became "enters"; "aura" became "feeling"; "takes place" became "happens"; "mythology" became "body of myths," etc. In two other instances the order of the words was reversed: "creation, nature, and death" became "creation, death, and nature" and the order of "basic nature of being" was reversed with "society's world view." Both the paraphrased passage and the directly quoted passages so carefully documented in the original were used here without any documentation. As written, this passage is almost purely a word-for-word copy of the source, retaining even the sentence structure and organization of the original. Even the use of a footnote could not save this paragraph from being condemned.

PATCHWORK PLAGIARISM

I was attracted to mythology because of my childhood fascination with the dramatic action of the magic-like stories they contain. Now, in college I realize that there is another level to the marvelous tales; they are metaphorical expressions of essential aspects of the human condition. All cultures seem to have a mythology that helps them understand the basic experiences of their existence. Even though many of these myths could never be scientifically proved, they do seem to parallel the meaning of a society's belief. **When people attempt to explain the unknown, they use archetypal images which come out of inner experiences. *I realized too that some of these images can be found in primitive art which is not radically distinct from language which shows that the underlying concepts of myth and art are similar because they both express the same subject matter which changes but whose nature is the same. My paper will investigate the common denominators of the verbal and visual expressions of these ideas and I will compare their metaphoric forms.

COMMENT: Changing a single word in a passage otherwise quoted verbatim does not produce a paraphrase. The starred passage (**) would still need to be in quotation marks and footnoted; the changes you make within a quoted passage should go in square brackets, as do all editorial changes and additions; ellipsis marks are used to indicate omissions from the source being quoted. Thus the starred (*) sentence above should be: I realized too that some of these images can be "found in primitive art . . . [which] is not radically distinct from language" according to Mitchell, which shows, Elizabeth Abel says "that the underlying concepts of myth and art are similar." The footnote number would then follow the quotation marks.

When whole phrases are lifted out and are put into a framework of your own wording or into a "different" arrangement of the original, the result is also called plagiarism. In the example given, the underlined phrases are lifted verbatim from the original. Though you would never be expected to put quotation marks merely around such phrases as "I realized," "when people attempt to explain," or "inner experiences," since they are part of our common idiom, you could not write such a sentence as the one marked ** and call it your own. This "rearrangement" is not really a paraphrasing. The sentence preceding it might be called a paraphrase but would still need a footnote; it is very awkwardly stated because the implications of the idea expressed were obviously not very clear to the writer. If all the underlined phrases were in quotation marks, the paragraph would resemble an old-fashioned patchwork quilt. It would also be quite unreadable and certainly not original. Not only is Markman not given credit for her work in the plagiarized version, but the sources *she* carefully documented have also been plagiarized.

"LIFTING OUT THE PERFECT PHRASES"

The aura of magic that pervades mythology and my early fascination with the dramatic action of the stories stimulated my interest in myths. That they were metaphorical expressions explaining creation, nature, and death was clear to me as I became more sophisticated. As metaphors they could by analogy capture the essential truth that was close to each social group so that it could understand the basic experiences of its existence. The imagery, when people attempt to explain the unknown comes from their own worldly experiences or from archetypal images that are part of their inner psyches as we find from illustrations found on maps of antiquity. Since art is not radically distinct from language,[1] I would like to investigate the common denominators of the insights of primitive people as they expressed them verbally in their myths and visually in their art to see if the nature is the same and to study the metaphoric forms of each of them.

---

[1]W. J. T. Mitchell, "Spatial Form in Literature: Towards a General Theory," *The Language of Images*, ed. W. J. T. Mitchell (Chicago: The University of Chicago Press, 1980) 296.

COMMENT: Though more subtle and clever, this kind of plagiarism is similar to the preceding patchwork illustration. The "perfect phrases" irresistible to the writer here are underlined so you may spot them easily. However, the order in which they appear is often altered.

The words that are underlined with wavy lines might be called paraphrases but could not be used without footnotes. The phrasing "the insights of primitive people as they expressed them verbally in their myths and visually in their art" certainly reflects Markman's idea and, though paraphrased, must be documented as having been quoted from Markman.

Two other serious errors were made in this paragraph:

1. Mitchell was cited in a footnote as if his article were a source used by the writer. (If you did not read the article, you may not cite it.)

2. Not content with "lifting" material from the Preface, the writer has copied the words "found on maps of antiquity" from Marie-Louise von Franz so carefully quoted in Markman's footnotes.

PARAPHRASE

PREFACE

My earliest attraction to mythology was based on a fascination with the

Myths fascinate on several levels. They are

dramatic action of the narratives and the aura of magic that pervades the

imaginative stories that have magic appeal.

world in which that action takes place. But gradually I realized that on

Moreover, the sophisticated scholar can see that

another level those marvelous tales were metaphorical expressions of

by their imagery they are able to capture the essence

essential aspects of the human condition. Each social group had obviously

of some of humanity's most important experiences,

developed a mythology by which it could understand the basic experiences

including how people came into being, their

of its existence, such as creation, nature, and death. Although their

relationship to the world around them, and death.

mythological stories might not be literally true, they do by analogy capture

Apparently every society develops a body of myths in order

the essential truth both of the society's world view and of the basic nature of

to understand these basic mysteries of life. Even though

being. Von Franz says that when people attempt to explain the unknown,

there is no way to prove anything scientifically, the central

they are likely to depend on imagery from what they do know or on

metaphors of the stories do express the essence of

archetypal images which come out of their own inner experiences.[1]

truth about the human condition. In her book about

Later I realized that these images are also found in primitive art. Mitchell

creation myths, for example, Marie Louise von Franz

explains that visual representation is "not radically distinct from language,"[2]

says that the metaphors are based on imagery either

and Elizabeth Abel contends that the underlying concepts of myth and art

from people's own experiences or from the primordial images of their psyches, and both W. J. T. Mitchell and Elizabeth Abel suggest that the same imagery

are similar in that both express a "common inner source whose subject

is often found in art forms even though the actual

matter changes but whose nature is the same."[3] I was challenged to

subject may not be the same. ② A comparison of the

investigate the common denominators of the verbal and visual expressions

two forms of expression would result in a very

of these insights and to do a comparative study of their metaphoric forms.

valuable study to discover the "truths" expressed in the metaphoric imagery that primitive societies have left us in their art and in their mythology.

---

[1]Marie-Louise von Franz, *Patterns of Creativity Mirrored in Creation Myths* (Zürich, Spring Publications, 1978) 5. Von Franz bases her conclusions on the images she has found on maps of antiquity.

[2]W. J. T. Mitchell, "Spatial Form in Literature: Toward a General Theory," *The Language of Images*, ed. W. J. T. Mitchell (Chicago: The University of Chicago Press, 1980) 296. Mitchell reinforces his point with a quote from Ludwig Wittgenstein's *Philosophical Investigations*: "A picture held us captive. And we could not get outside it, for it lay in our language and language seemed to repeat it to us inexorably" (Mitchell 271).

[3]Elizabeth Abel, "Redefining the Sister Arts: Baudelaire's Response to the Art of Delacroix," *The Language of Images*, ed. W. J. T. Mitchell (Chicago: The University of Chicago Press, 1980) 41.

> [1] Marie-Louise von Franz, *Patterns of Creativity Mirrored in Creation Myths* (Zürich: Spring Publications, 1978), 5; quoted in Roberta H. Markman, "The Metaphoric Vision in Mythology and Art," master's thesis, California State University Long Beach, 1982, iv.
>
> [2] W.J.T. Mitchell, "Spatial Form in Literature: Toward a General Theory" and Elizabeth Abel, "Redefining the Sister Arts: Baudelaire's Response to the Art of Delacroix," both in *The Language of Images*, ed. W.J.T. Mitchell (Chicago: The University of Chicago Press, 1980), 41, 271; quoted in Roberta H. Markman, "The Metaphoric Vision in Mythology and Art," master's thesis, California State University, Long Beach, 1982, iv.

COMMENT: This is a paraphrase, for the writer here has followed the source, sentence by sentence and idea by idea but has used his or her own words. There is value in doing this (see the reasons listed preceding card C on pp. 69 to 70), but remember that you must not alter the sense of the original.

          Also remember: although the words in a paraphrase (or a précis) may be truly your own, the thoughts and opinions are not; therefore you must acknowledge your indebtedness to the thinking of the original writer by giving your source in a parenthetical reference or footnote. (*See* STEP 9.)

REMEMBER: Of the four preceding examples, only the paraphrase could be used without quotation marks, and even it would require documentation. THE OTHER EXAMPLES WOULD BE CALLED PLAGIARISM *EVEN WITH* DOCUMENTATION.

THE LIBRARY: A STEP TO MASTER

USING THE LIBRARY FOR BOOKS AND OTHER COMMUNICATIONS MEDIA

The library is the most valuable storehouse of information on almost every subject for anyone doing research. It is essential, therefore, to become familiar with the tools in your library and to make use of as many of them as your time affords.

1. The Online Card Catalog (or OPAC)

All students should consider the online catalog (or OPAC) as their most valuable index. When you locate an entry for a book you want, it is essential to copy the entire call number accurately, since it is the most important mark of identification for locating any book. Remember to bring a pen and paper or a jump drive to store the information.

2. Internet Searches

These searches enable students to conduct their own search of the databases that exist in a particular area of study. Depending on the database you use, you can search for a bibliographic list or a full text of the articles. This is the fastest means of establishing your preliminary bibliography. (See STEP 4, pp. 18 to 23.)

3. The Reference Section

Become familiar with the basic reference tools in your particular subject. The periodical indexes, special indexes, bibliographies, and special encyclopedias (see pages 152 to 159) are in the reference room of the library. Ask at the information desk to find out whether or not the library has reference rooms for different subjects or whether all references may be found in one place.

4. Media Center

Many libraries afford students the opportunity to view films, DVDs, and videotapes; often, arrangements must be made in advance for this privilege. In addition, the media center will often include audio materials such as phonograph records, audiotapes, CD's and MP3 or .WAV files.

5. Microfilms and Microfiche

Although most materials once available on microfilm and microfiche have been digitized, some materials may still exist in your library only in the microfilm or microfiche format for a number of reasons. If you think you may need access to these materials, ask a librarian for assistance.

6. Periodicals

Many periodical indexes are available in the reference room of the library or online. (See pages 152 to 159.) After you have found the source of an article that interests you, check the holding file of periodicals to find out if the periodical you need is available in your library. Issues of periodicals published in the same year have the same volume number and are eventually bound together in the same volume; so if you need several issues with the same volume number (of a bound periodical), you need to ask or look for only one bound volume. Often you can arrange to borrow those that are not available in your library, but this entails using the interlibrary loan service discussed under 13d following.

7. Special Services

Your library is often equipped to offer you many special services:

a. Renewal of books you have not finished using.

b. "Holding" or "recalling" a book that someone else has taken out of the library. If you request a "hold" on a book, your library will notify you when it is returned to the library. It is important to respond quickly to a notice that a "hold" book is waiting for you because your library may have a time limit on this service.

c. Xerox or copying machines are usually available for you to use in copying material from a book in the library. Be aware of the copyright laws, however, as only a limited amount of material is legally available for copying.

d. Most libraries subscribe to an interlibrary loan service, which makes available most of the world's materials, even those not in your library. Materials obtained through this service are usually borrowed for a very limited time, so it is wise to find out how long it will take for the material to reach you and how long you may keep it.

There are, of course, many ways in which you will encounter the names of books or periodicals that you think will be valuable for your research. Usually you will find them in bibliographies by other researchers or referred to in foot-notes or appendixes in your sources. Then you should check the Worldcat (*www.worldcat.org*), where you can locate books and periodicals in thousands of American libraries. Through the interlibrary loan service you can usually obtain them.

e. Computers and printers are available for student use in most libraries.

8. The Reference Librarian

The reference librarian is professionally trained to help you locate materials and use the library to its greatest potential. Solicit the help of a reference librarian only after you have tried to help yourself, but do not hesitate to ask for help when you honestly need it.

APPENDIXES

APPENDIX A:
RESEARCH TERMS DEFINED

Research writing, like any other specialized activity, has its own jargon. The following are terms frequently used by people in discussing research:

abridgment: a condensation of the author's original work.

acknowledgment: recognition made of indebtedness to another.

annotated bibliography: a bibliography with comments about each source, telling how inclusive it is, how valuable it is, what the author does and what his or her purpose is, and so on.

authority: a writer whose work and opinions are generally accepted as final and reliable.

autobiography: the writer's own account of his or her life.

bibliography: a list of books, articles, and other material about a single subject, idea, person, and so forth.

biography: a writer's account of the life story of another. There are three types: straight, fictional, and critical.

brackets: the punctuation marks [ ] used only within a quoted passage to enclose additions in your own words (called editorial comment, insertion, or interpolation) explaining a word or giving information needed by the reader. Never use unnecessary brackets: "He [Aristotle] wrote an early definition of tragedy"; simply write this: Aristotle "wrote an early definition of tragedy." Parentheses are different and have a different function.

card catalog: a card file listing alphabetically all books in a library.

compile (compilation, compiler): to combine related material. The one who does the combining is a compiler; the result is a compilation.

cross-reference: words or symbols that refer the reader to other places where information about an idea may be found.

Cross-references are used in card catalogs, footnotes, indexes, and bibliographies.

database: a collection of information, often limited to a certain subject area, either in print or electronic form.

dedication: a page of tribute by the writer to one he or she admires or feels indebted to or wants to honor.

dissertation: a long, involved, and formal exposition on some serious or scholarly subject.

In academic circles, the word is usually reserved for those papers written by a candidate for a doctorate; the word *thesis* indicates the paper written by a candidate for the master's degree.

document: to acknowledge indebtedness for an idea or fact. It is necessary to document the source of any critical opinion (and some facts); see STEP 9.

ellipsis: an omission within quoted material indicated by three periods with a space before, after, and between periods (. . .).

The ellipsis marks may indicate the omission of a single word or of whole sentences, but you must never omit words that would change the essential, intended meaning of the quoted material. It is illogical to use an ellipsis to open or to close a quoted passage; hence it would never come immediately after an opening quotation mark nor immediately before the closing quotation mark unless you wish to emphasize the omission of material before or after the passage quoted; it should be used only to show an omission within a quoted passage. Use a fourth period only before a new sentence which begins after an ellipsis within the quoted passage.

endnote: a documentary note placed at the end of a section, chapter, paper, or book rather than at the bottom of the page on which the note number appears.

footnote: a documentary note placed at the bottom of the page on which the note number appears.

foreword: a note from the author at the front of a book.

Current practice reveals that there is some confusion about the exact distinctions between the sections called *foreword*, *preface*, and *introduction*; however, by whatever name it may be called, this section sets forth an explanation by the author of his or her intended purpose and reason for writing as well as any information or background that might be needed by the reader.

Internet address: a description of the location of an item on the Internet, this address enables a user to reach the specified item.

Internet browser: a software program which enables a user to use Internet tools such as a search engine.

Internet domain: one of the networks, such as *.edu* or *.com*, which make up the Internet.

interpolate: to insert an idea or material or information where it should logically go in the organization of the writing.

introduction: a section that follows the table of contents and introduces the work that follows. See *foreword*.

online computer catalog: the computer system used to duplicate or replace the card catalog; see *card catalog*.

pagination: the system for numbering pages of a manuscript or book.

parentheses: the punctuation marks ( ) used to enclose your own explanatory material or words interpolated into a sentence or phrase of your own.

Brackets enclose material more foreign to the context than that put in parentheses; avoid the overuse of either.

parenthetical reference: a documentary note placed within parentheses immediately after the material being documented indicating the source of that material.

plagiarism: a literary word for the thievery of style, ideas, or phrasing.

Plagiarism ranges from the theft of a single word to the deliberate copying (without quotation marks) of a whole passage; it can be avoided by careful note-taking and footnoting (q.v.); everything not documented must be your own original idea and phrasing. You are not writing original sentences of your own if you merely arrange into a new order or sentence pattern some select phrases and sentences taken without quotation marks from your sources. See section entitled "Plagiarism: A Step to Avoid," pages 109 to 116.

preface: a note from the author which comes before (some put it after) the table of contents or outline.

The preface is frequently followed by a page of acknowledgments; see *foreword*.

primary source: the literature, the work, manuscript, journal, letters, and so on as originally written.

A secondary source is a work written about an original source; a primary source in connection with one subject might be a secondary source in connection with another subject.

For example, a novel by Faulkner would be a primary source for a paper about Faulkner or the novel in America and so on; a Master's thesis on Faulkner would be a primary source for a paper on the writing of theses in American colleges and universities, but it would be a secondary source for a paper on Faulkner.

reference or reference book: any source being read for information. The number and quality of your references will in large measure determine the quality of your finished paper.

rough draft: the first and any subsequent writing before the paper is put in final form.

Rough drafts are subject to drastic and sometimes numerous revisions.

scan: to make a cursory reading of material in order to evaluate it and decide how to read it.

secondary source: a criticism or evaluation of an original piece of writing. See *primary source.*

thesis: the simple statement of opinion which the entire work is designed to support.

See complete explanation and examples in STEP 3.

URL: Internet address, defined previously.

APPENDIX B:
USING FOOTNOTES OR ENDNOTES
(Chicago Format)

Decide where you are going to put your documentation; there are two acceptable places. Endnotes are placed after the text of the research paper or chapter. Start them on a new page entitled Notes numbered in sequence with the preceding page. Footnotes, on the other hand, are placed at the bottom of the page on which the footnote number occurred in the text. The first footnote begins four lines (two double spaces) after the last line of the text. You can make a line on the third line above by striking the underline key fifteen times and then double space before writing the footnote number. Endnotes are generally simpler and preferable unless you are instructed otherwise, or unless you are using a computer program that will do the spacing, numbering, and form for your footnotes and/or your endnotes.

PROCEDURE FOR WRITING FOOTNOTES OR ENDNOTES

1. Take out the bibliography card from which your material came.

2. Write your footnote or endnote as you would a sentence; do not separate into lines as you did on the bibliography card.

3. Write the number of the note in either of two ways, but be consistent:

   a. above the line as it must be in the text or

   b. on the same line as the note will be.

   For the former, use no period after the number; for the latter, be sure to use a period and two spaces before beginning your note. Check to see that the number in the text matches the number given for the note. Remember that notes are numbered consecutively throughout the paper; there will be only one note numbered 1 in any short paper (fewer than fifty typewritten pages) or for each chapter in a long paper.

4. Indent the note number and first line as for a paragraph; bring the second and each succeeding line of the same note back to the margin of the text.

5. Fill in all information from the bibliography card exactly as it is written with these exceptions:

   a. write the author's name in regular order (not reversed) followed by a comma, not a period;

   b. omit the period after the name of a book; put a comma instead of a period after the name of an article;

   c. enclose within parentheses the publication facts for a book (city, publisher, date), omitting the period after the date.

6. Copy exactly the page number from which the material came. If a pamphlet or booklet has no page number, supply a page number in brackets or write the words *no page* after the comma.

7. Put a period at the end of the note.

8. Before you put your bibliography card away, put a check mark on the bottom left corner to remind yourself that you have used this source once for a first-entry footnote and that it must be included in your final bibliography.

9. All future references to this source or to any other source already documented in full will be in second-entry footnote form. See p. 137.

FOOTNOTE OR ENDNOTE FORMS

The following examples show the footnote form for each of the bibliography cards and entries used in STEP 4, pages 23 to 48.

FORMS FOR FIRST ENTRY FOOTNOTES OR ENDNOTE
From a Print Media Source that Is Not Part of a Larger Work

NOTE: When typing your own footnotes remember that you will underline all items that appear in italics. Of course, if you are using a computer, you will use the *italics* font.

Some writers do not include in footnotes all of the publication data if a bibliography is given at the end of the paper; however, many colleges do require the following full form as well as a bibliography.

1. the basic form

[1]Joseph Campbell, *The Inner Reaches of Outer Space: Metaphor as Myth and as Religion* (New York: Alfred van der Marck Editions, 1986) 28.

2. no author

[2]*Máscaras Mexicanas: de la Colección del Ing. Victor José Moya* (México: Dirección de Museos del Instituto Nacional de Antropología e Historia, 1974) 97–99.

3. two authors

[3]Roberta H. Markman and Peter T. Markman, *The Flayed God: The Mesoamerican Mythological Tradition* (San Francisco: Harper San Francisco, 1992) 36.

4. three authors

[4]Johanna Broda, Davíd Carrasco, and Eduardo Matos Moctezuma, *The Great Temple of Tenochtitlan: Center and Periphery in the Aztec World* (Berkeley: University of California Press, 1987) 112.

5. more than three authors

[5]Samuel K. Lothrop and others, *Essays in Pre-Columbian Art and Archaeology* (Cambridge, Massachusetts: Harvard UP, 1961) 47.

6. corporate authorship

[6]Instituto Guerrerense de la Cultura, *Calendario de Fiestas del Estado de Guerrero* (Chilpancingo, Guerrero, México: Instituto Guerrerense de la Cultura, 1987) 22.

7. an author and an editor

[7]Joseph Campbell, *The Power of Myth* with Bill Moyers, ed. Betty Sue Flowers (New York: Doubleday, 1988) 78–79.

8. an author and a translator

[8]Mircea Eliade, *Images and Symbols*, trans. Philip Mairet (Kansas City, Missouri: Sheed Andrews and McMeel, 1961) 152.

9. an author, an editor, and a translator

[9]Pablo Neruda, *A New Decade (Poems: 1958–1967)*, ed. Ben Belitt, trans. Ben Belitt and Alastair Reid (New York: Grove Press, 1969) 105.

10. an editor but no author

[10]Diane Apostolos-Cappadona, ed., *Symbolism, the Sacred, and the Arts* (New York: Crossroad, 1988) ix.

NOTE: This form would be used to refer to a section of the anthology other than one of the individually titled pieces, as well as for any other book with an editor but no author; for a reference to an essay in this anthology, see example 28 following.

11. a translator and an editor but no author

[11]Thelma D. Sullivan, trans., *A Scattering of Jades: Stories, Poems, and Prayers of the Aztecs*, ed. T. J. Knab (New York: Simon and Schuster, 1994) 68.

12. a compiler

[12]Curt Muser, comp., *Facts and Artifacts of Ancient Middle America* (New York: E. P. Dutton, 1978) 44.

13. one volume in a multivolume set when all volumes have the same title

[13]E. A. Wallis Budge, *The Gods of the Egyptians or Studies in Egyptian Mythology* (1904; rpt. New York: Dover Publications, 1969) 2:361.

NOTE: The volume number, 2, appears before the colon and the page number, 361, appears after.
This book is a modern reprint of an older edition; see example 18.

14. one volume in a multivolume set when each volume has a separate title

[14]Michael D. Coe and Richard A. Diehl, *The People of the River*, vol. 2 of *In the Land of the Olmec* (Austin: University of Texas Press, 1980) 119.

15. a book in a series edited by one other than the author

[15]David Maclagen, *Creation Myths: Man's Introduction to the World*, in the *Art and Imagination* series, ed. Jill Purce (London: Thames and Hudson, 1977) 112–115.

16. a book with a subtitle or secondary title

[16]Vincent F. Hopper ed. and trans. *Chaucer's Canterbury Tales: An Interlinear Translation* (Woodbury, New York: Barron's 1970) 17.

NOTE: Obviously Chaucer did not write a book with this title; therefore this entry is correct for this book. However, if you quoted the lines from Chaucer with the older spelling, your footnote would be thus:
[16]Geoffrey Chaucer, "The Pardoner's Tale," *Chaucer's Canterbury Tales: An Interlinear Translation*, ed. and trans. Vincent F. Hopper (Woodbury, New York: Barron's, 1970) 299.

17. an edition subsequent to the first edition

[17]Michael D. Coe, *The Maya*, 5th ed. (New York: Thames and Hudson, 1993) 29.

18. a modern reprint of an older edition

[18]Frances Toor, *Mexican Popular Arts* (1939; rpt. Detroit: Blaine Ethridge Books, 1973) 106.

19. a pamphlet, bulletin, manual, or monograph

[19]Lenore H. Mulryan, *Mexican Figural Ceramists and Their Work*, Monograph Series, no. 16 (Los Angeles: Museum of Cultural History, University of California, Los Angeles, 1982) 16.

20. a catalog of an exhibition

[20]Erika Billeter, ed., *The Blue House: The World of Frida Kahlo*, an exhibit at the Schirn Kunsthalle, Frankfurt, March 6–May 23, 1993 and The Museum of Fine Arts, Houston, June 6–August 29, 1993 (Frankfurt: Schirn Kunsthalle and Houston: Museum of Fine Arts, 1993) 11.

21. a government document

[21]U.S. Congressional Record, 80th Cong., 2nd Sess., 1948, XCII, Part 6, 5539.

22. a dictionary

[22]*Webster's New Collegiate Dictionary* (Springfield, Massachusetts: G. & C. Merriam Company, 1984).

NOTE: No page number is required since the dictionary is arranged alphabetically.

From a Print Media Source Contained Within a Larger Work

23. the basic form

[23]Gregory S. Jay, "Knowledge, Power, and the Struggle for Representation," *College English* January 1994: 12.

24. a periodical article with no author

[24]"The Presidential Policy Scoreboard," *The World and I* June 1988: 52–55.

25. a titled book review

[25]Octavio Paz, "Food of the Gods," trans. Eliot Weinberger, review of *The Blood of Kings* by Linda Schele and Mary Ellen Miller, *The New York Review of Books* 26 February 1987: 3–7.

26. an untitled book review

[26]Franke J. Neumann, review of *Masks of the Spirit: Image and Metaphor in Mesoamerica* by Peter T. Markman and Roberta H. Markman, *Religious Studies Review* April 1993: 179.

27. a newspaper article or editorial

[27]Dan Williams, "400-Year Church Ties Cut by Ancient Mexican Tribe," *Los Angeles Times* 5 July 1987: I:1.

NOTE: For an unsigned article, you would begin with the title of the article. I:1 indicates that the information to which you are referring is on page 1 of section I.

28. an essay (or other work) written by one person in an anthology edited by another

[28]Mircea Eliade, "The Symbolism of Shadows in Archaic Religions," *Symbolism, the Sacred, and the Arts*, ed. Diane Apostolos-Cappadona (New York: Crossroads, 1988) 5.

29. an encyclopedia article

[29]Kees W. Bolle, "Myth and Mythology: The Nature, Functions, and Types of Myth," *The New Encyclopaedia Britannica: Macropaedia*, 15th ed., 1986, 24:713.

NOTE: For an unsigned article, you would begin with the title of the article. Remember that most articles are signed with intials only; you must look at the beginning of the first volume to find the author's full name.

30. an introduction or limited part of a book by one other than the author

[30]Joseph Campbell, "Introduction," *Masks of the Spirit: Image and Metaphor in Mesoamerica*, Peter T. Markman and Roberta H. Markman (Berkeley: University of California Press, 1989) xv.

31. author of a work in a book in a series edited by others

[31]Jack Waardenburg, "Symbolic Aspects of Myth," *Myth, Symbol, and Reality*, ed. Alan M. Olson, vol. 1 of The Boston University Studies in Philosophy and Religion, ed. Leroy S. Rouner (Notre Dame, Indiana: University of Notre Dame Press, 1980) 53.

32. a reprint with critical comment by the editor

[32]Andrew Wright, "Afterword," Joyce Cary, *The Horse's Mouth* (1944; rtp. New York: Harper & Row/Perennial Library, 1965) 349.

33. a casebook (a text for controlled research)

[33]David Stevenson, "J. D. Salinger: The Mirror of Crisis," *The Nation*, 9 March 1957: 215; rpt. *If You Really Want to Know: A*

Catcher Casebook, ed. Malcolm M. Marsden (Chicago: Scott, Foresman, 1963) 22.

NOTE: There are two ways to use a casebook: as an anthology of essays about a particular subject or as a library containing essays, which you will read and document as if you were reading the original. For the latter use, the original pagination appears in the casebook with slash marks wherever a page change occurred in the original. Check with your instructor about how to use the casebook, but it would never be wrong to use this model form.

From Other Types of Print Media Sources

34. an interview

[34]Roberta H. Markman, Professor of Comparative Literature, California State University, Long Beach, personal interview on Mexican masks, Long Beach, California, 16 April 1994.

NOTE: Unless the person interviewed is well known, you should indicate through the use of the person's title why he or she is an authority on the subject of the interview.

35. an unpublished lecture

[35]Peter T. Markman, Professor of English, Fullerton College, class lecture on Carlos Fuentes, *The Death of Artemio Cruz*, Fullerton College, Fullerton, California, 3 May 1992.

36. a published lecture

[36]Kurt Vonnegut, Jr., "Address to Graduating Class at Bennington College, 1970," *Wampeters, Foma and Granfalloons (Opinions)* (New York: Dell, 1976) 163.

37. photocopied material

[37]Betty Ann Brown, "Fiestas de Oaxaca," 1977 (mimeographed) 3.

38. an unpublished thesis or dissertation

[38]Roberta H. Markman, "Mann's Joseph: From Dreamer to Artist," diss., Occidental College, Los Angeles, 1969, 308.

39. a letter

[39]Unpublished letter from Ernest Hemingway to Roberta Hoffman, dated August 12, 1957.

40. The Bible or any well-known literary work that can be identified by book or scene plus lines or by chapter and verse

[40]I Corinthians 13:12, The Bible, Revised Standard Version.

NOTE: The names of sacred scripture are neither underlined nor put in quotation marks. The translation of the Bible is assumed to be the King James Version unless another is named, as in the preceding example.

[40]John Milton, *Paradise Lost*, bk. I, ll. 13–14.

NOTE: The particular edition you used is not needed unless the work is a translation.

The name of a novel, play, or long poem would be underlined even if it is part of an anthology.

41. an abridgment

[41]*Style Manual* (abridged), rev. ed. (Washington, D.C.: Government Printing Office, 1984) 19.

42. record jacket notes

[42]Gustav Mahler, *Symphony No. 4*, Concertgebouw Orchestra, Amsterdam, cond. Bernard Haitink (Philips, SAL 3729 802 888 LY), jacket notes.

43. a pamphlet included with a record

[43]Richard Kostelanetz and Editors of Time-Life Records, "A Listener's Guide to the Recordings," *The Music of Today* in *The Story of Great Music* series (Time-Life Records, STL 145) 3.

From an Electronic Media Source That Is Not Part of a Larger Work

44. the basic form

[44]D. L. Ashliman, ed. and trans., *Folklore and Mythology Electronic Texts* (1996–2000, University of Pittsburgh), 1 January 2001 <*http://www.pitt.edu/~dash/folktexts.html*>.

45. online information database

[45]Gregory Crane, ed., *The Perseus Digital Library* (Tufts University), 3 January 2001 <*http://www.perseus.tufts.edu/ indexplain.html*>.

46. Internet site maintained by an individual or group

[46]Sherwood School Students, *Building the Windy City*, 27 December 2000 <*http://library.thinkquest.org /j002846*>.

47. online book (with an author and a translator)

[47]Euripides, *Alcestis*, trans. David Kovacs, *The Perseus Digital Library* (Tufts University) (Cambridge, MA: Harvard University Press, in press.), 26 December 2000 <*http://www.perseus.tufts. edu/cgi-bin/ptext?doc=perseus%3atext%3a1999.01.0088*> episode 4.

48. e-mail from a source to you

[48]Armando Colina, Director, Galeria Arvil, Mexico City <*colina@conecta.com.mx*>, *Re Frida*, e-mail to Peter T. Markman, 12 December 2000.

49. posting to an electronic bulletin board or discussion group

[49]L. Poirier, *This Site*, 11 June 1999, Genesis Discussion, 29 December 2000 <*http://library.thinkquest.org/29064/cgi-bin/ ultraboard/ultraboard.pl?action=showpost&board=feed&post= 1&idle=7&sort=0&order=descend&page=)&session=*>.

From an Electronic Media Source Contained Within a Larger Work

50. the basic form

[50]Susan M. Ryan, "Melville, Race, and the Ambiguities of Violence," *American Literary History* Winter 2000, 22 December 2000 <*http://muse.jhu.edu/journals/alh/joc/alh12.4.html*>.

51. an article in an online periodical

[51]Daniel   Chamberlain   "Bookmarks: Less   Is   More," *Themestream* 30 September 2000, 7 December 2000 <*http:// www.themestream.com/gspd_browse/browse/view_article.gsp?c_id= 195850&id_list=&cookied=t*>.

52. a book review

[52]Michael Gorra, "After the Fall," Review of *Disgrace* by J. M. Coetzee, *The New York Times on the Web* 28 November 1999, 6 December 2000 <*http://www.nytimes.com/books/99/11/28/reviews/ 99128.28gorrat.html*>.

53. a newspaper article or editorial

[53]J. M. Coetzee, "Into the Dark Chamber: The Novelist and South Africa," *The New York Times on the Web* 12 January 1986, 29 December 2000 <*http://www.nytimes.com/books/97/11/02/ home/coetzee-chamber.html*>.

54. a work written by one person in an anthology edited by another

[54]Hans Christian Andersen, "Yggdrasil," *Folklore and Mythology Electronic Texts*, ed. and trans. D. L. Ashliman (1996–2000, University of Pittsburgh), 3 December 2000 <*http://www.pitt.edu/ ~dash/yggdrasil.html*>.

55. an encyclopedia article

[55]"Whitman," *The Cambridge History of English and American Literature in 18 Volumes*, 1907–1921, vol. 16, 2 January 2001 <*http://www.bartleby.com/226/1607.html*>.

From Other Types of Electronic Media Sources

56. a CD-ROM or DVD

[56]*Perseus 2.0: Interactive Sources and Studies on Ancient Greece* (New Haven: Yale UP, 1996), CD-ROM, 4 discs: disc 2.

57. a record, audiotape, or compact disc

[57]Johannes Brahms, *Violin Sonatas Nos. 1–3*, Itzhak Perlman, violin, and Vladimir Ashkenazy, piano (EMI/Angel, CDC 7 47403 2, compact disc).

58. a film, videotape, or DVD

[58]*Wings of Desire*, Wim Wenders, director (Orion Pictures Corp., 1988).

59. a lecture on a record, tape, or compact disc

[59]Thomas Scherman, narrator, "Musical Program Notes," Beethoven's *Symphony No. 5 in C Minor, Op. 67*, The Philharmonic Promenade Orchestra of London, cond. Sir Adrian Boult (Vanguard, MARS 3005).

60. a radio program

[60]*Tribute: Ernest von Dohanyi*, KFAC (1330 AM, 92.3 FM), Los Angeles, 7–8 pm., 26 July 1998.

61. a television program

[61]*Moyers: Joseph Campbell and the Power of Myth*, pt. 1, KCET (Channel 28), Los Angeles, PBS, 10–11 pm., 23 May 1998.

62. computer software

[62]John A. Weyh, Joseph R. Crook, and Les N. Hauge, *The Mole Concept*, pt. 2 of *Concepts in General Chemistry*, IBM PC computer software (COMPress).

ABBREVIATED FORMS FOR SECOND-ENTRY FOOTNOTES

For every first-entry footnote (the first time you document information from a source) you will give the complete bibliographical information *plus* the exact page number, which you have already entered in the cutoff lines. See STEP 7, p. 79. For all succeeding footnotes referring to that source, use the second-entry form.

1. Current usage has eliminated Latin from footnotes. (See section of abbreviations on pp. 160 to 161 so that you will know what the Latin terms indicate when you see them used in older texts.) Current form now requires that for second-entry footnotes you give only enough to identify the source such as the author's name and page number:

Campbell 20–21.

2. If two or more works by the same author have been used, such as Campbell's *The Power of Myth* and his *The Inner Reaches of Outer Space: Metaphor as Myth and as Religion*, a shortened form of the title should follow the author's last name for all second-entry footnotes, such as Campbell, *Power* 31.

Campbell, *Inner* 20–21.

3. If two or more authors with the same last name have been used, the first name should be given, and if either one has two or more works cited in the paper, a short title must be given for each:

Joseph Campbell, *Inner* 48.

Joseph Campbell, *Power* 20–21.

Jack R. Campbell 42–46.

4. If you have a footnote referring to a source without an author:

"The Presidential Policy Scoreboard" 53.

A title may be shortened by using an ellipsis:

"The Presidential . . ." 53.

5. If reference information is given in the text, the second-entry footnote may simply include the information that is missing, such as the page number (if the author has been mentioned in connection with the information) or the title and page if there is more than one work by the author cited in the paper. However, it is not incorrect to repeat the author's name or the text in the note.

SAMPLE PAPER 2
USING ENDNOTE STYLE

Note that the references for this paper appear at the end of the paper as endnotes, but had they been placed at the bottom of each page as footnotes, the style and form for the references would be exactly the same.

Words and Pictures:
The Mythic Vision in Tales and Art

Human beings everywhere have always been curious. They look around their world, poke and pry into its features, in order to understand everything that confronts them. We can see evidence of this even in the oldest stories that have come down to us. In the epic of *Gilgamesh*, from the second or third millennium B.C., for example, as in the later story of creation in Genesis, people were challenged to "name" the animals and the other features of their world. This "naming" is significant on many levels, but in its most symbolic sense it signifies their coming to understand the basic nature of things. In fact, the Biblical account of creation makes clear that the development of that understanding is God's intention in setting the task of naming[1] and that the understanding involves an awareness of the relationship of what they have "named" to the "final, indivisible presence of Being itself,"[2] that is, to God, thereby understanding it in the most fundamental sense.

As this suggests, human beings have always known that the world they inhabit consists of more than observable reality, and their curiosity has always extended beyond what they could see or touch. The same early stories show us that such aspects of life as creation and death, aspects that exist beyond the realms of intellect and logic, were similarly named and thus understood. This "naming," however, has not always been verbal; the same need to understand is the most powerful impetus for the creation of visual art in traditional societies,[3] for such mythic art serves "to kindle into meaning [for human beings] aspects of their perception that would otherwise remain external to their minds."[4] The ability to "name" what had been unknown provides the psychological security that human beings have always sought.

The curious individual, whether of one of today's technologically sophisticated, urban societies or of a "primal"[5] society of the present or distant past, begins this search for understanding with a question, and that question triggers the search that leads ultimately to an understanding that can be communicated through the fashioning of a mythic story or image.[6] This is necessarily a process that begins in the individual since "the myths are metaphorical of spiritual potentiality in the [individual] human being, and the same powers that animate our life animate the life of the world."[7] The mythic images created as a result of the search express metaphorically the understanding that has been achieved, an understanding of the realm beyond the observable. Since myths and art use metaphors in that way to "speak about the unknowable in terms of the known,"[8] they are able to transmit the understanding of reality that results from the creative response to a confrontation with the unknown.[9]

Because they answer humanity's seemingly universal basic questions in particular ways, the myths define the cultures that create them,[10] and, conversely, they serve an important educational function in their community by expressing "the wisdom of life" as understood by that culture.[11] Pemberton illustrates this point in his discussion of the verses of the <u>Odu</u> recited by Ifa diviners of the African Yoruba culture. Through them he demonstrates that myth and art, by expressing the world view and values of their particular culture, explain the varying roles of human beings and the powers that shape their lives as well as help the Yoruba society understand how to cope with its problems.[12] Because myths serve such functions as these, there seems to be no question among scholars that myth is essential

to existence[13] or that "mere purposive rationality,"
on the other hand, "unaided by such phenomena as
art, religion, dream . . . is necessarily pathogenic
and destructive of life."[14]

Thus both mythology and mythic art create a kind
of cosmic order out of what appears to be chaos,[15]
and by so doing are clearly not the *opposite* of science[16] or less valuable than logic.[17] "Myths are fictional, to be sure, but that fictional need not mean
unreal and certainly not unempirical."[18] The great
myths, like great art, are concerned with capturing
the essence of their subjects. Dorothy Jean Ray
points this out in her discussion of an Eskimo mask
when she explains how the image on the mask captures
not an individual animal, "but the vital force representing a chain or continuum of all the individual
spirits of that genus which had lived, were living,
or were to live."[19] Its "truth," then, is not dependent on reproducing the details of a particular
visual reality. Going "beyond" the object in that
way permits a freedom from the limitations of the
"'historic moment.'"[20] It is in this sense that "the
artist penetrates—at times dangerously—into the
depths of the world and his own psyche,"[21] and it is
for this reason and in this way that "the artist . . .
brings the images of a mythology to manifestation;
without images (whether mental or visual) there is
no mythology."[22]

These images may be expressed either in words or
graphically, and scholars have compared the verbally
expressed mythology and the visually expressed
mythic art of primal societies by considering their
methodologies as well as their functions and thematic concerns. Human beings think in images and,
according to von Franz, "the only reality we can
talk about . . . is the *image* of reality in our field of
consciousness."[23] Thus Jacques Waardenburg can say
that a myth "can be called a 'moving symbolism.'"[24]
Others have also investigated this relationship.
Cassirer points out that "word magic is everywhere
accompanied by picture magic,"[25] and Abel shows that

both narrative myths and mythic art express a "common inner source whose subject matter changes but whose nature is the same."[26]

Ultimately, however, there is no doubt that

> the relationship between word and image is, potentially, at once metonymic[27] and metaphoric: metonymic in that the two complete each other sequentially and as parts of a whole: metaphoric in that each translates into the other's medium. Ideally, image melts into speech, speech crystallizes the immediacy of the image.[28]

Thus it is primarily as metaphors that art and mythology are able to serve as "poetic expressions of . . . transcendental seeing."[29] By bringing together "*two frames of reference* of which the reader [or viewer] must be simultaneously aware,"[30] both art and mythology "bring truth into being"[31] and serve the essential functions that have been attributed to them. By juxtaposing everyday experiences to the images of imagination, the mundane is metaphorically transformed into a revelation of the "'extraordinary' aspects of ordinary reality."[32] As he wears a mask or plays out his mythology in a ritual, "the man of the archaic societies becomes conscious of himself in an 'open world' that is rich in meaning,"[33] detaching himself from his narrow environment.[34] It follows, then, that "'to live' a symbol [in ritual] and to decipher the messages [of ritual and myth] correctly is equivalent to gaining access to the universal."[35]

For traditional societies if the images created by the visual and verbal arts are not "the vessels of spiritual revelation," they fail as art and become mere "things."[36] It is the very nature and power of the metaphor that keep art and mythology from becoming "things." By creating and maintaining the tension between the known and the unknown, the conscious and the unconscious, the outer and the inner, the past and the present, "the metaphor has

the task of destroying the rigid reduction and limitations of the word"[37] and of bringing two images
together in a process that remains "eternally alive
and universally accessible";[38] yet it must, as David
Attenborough says of a Dogon sculpture, "be understood in its own terms,"[39] as it would have been by
its creator. In myth "the word [or image] speaks as
if vested with its own authority,"[40] for "myths convey what a culture has chosen as its most important
symbolic interpretations."[41]

Clearly then, "images, symbols and myths are not
irresponsible creations of the psyche; they respond
to a need and fulfill a function, that of bringing to
light the most hidden modalities of being."[42] "Reaching into depths into which our daily life with its
various rituals can scarcely follow,"[43] they capture
the essence of the human condition and force us to
realize that the human race cannot be divided into
"primitives" and moderns; there is a unity in the
structure of humanity, and no one group can be considered inferior to another.[44] "The needs, aspirations, and longings of mankind are similar,"[45] and as
we investigate the various manifestations of the
human attempt to understand the basic phenomena of
life through the metaphorical expression of insights,
both visually in art and verbally in mythology, we
will find that they speak to all people in "a language of vision which may tell us things about ourselves . . . that words alone cannot touch."[46] They will
fulfill what Joseph Campbell calls "the most essential
service of a mythology," that "of opening the mind
and heart to the utter wonder of all being."[47]

ENDNOTES

[1]Genesis 1:26 and 2:19, The Bible, Revised Standard Version.

[2]Willard Gingerich, "Heidegger and the Aztecs: The Poetics of Knowing in Pre-Hispanic Nahuatl Poetry," *Recovering the Word: Essays on Native American Literature*, ed. Brian Swann and Arnold Krupat (Berkeley: University of California Press, 1987) 109.

[3]Paul S. Wingert, *Primitive Art: Its Traditions and Styles* (New York: New American Library, 1962) 30.

[4]Joshua C. Taylor, "Two Visual Excursions," *The Language of Images*, ed. W. J. T. Mitchell (Chicago: The University of Chicago Press, 1980) 31.

[5]Following Jamake Highwater's suggestion (*The Primal Mind: Vision and Reality in Indian America* [New York: Harper & Row, 1981] xix), I will use *primal* instead of *primitive* when discussing technologically undeveloped traditional cultures to avoid the negative connotations of the latter term.

[6]Mircea Eliade, *Images and Symbols*, trans. Philip Mairet (Kansas City, Missouri: Sheed Andrews and McMeel, 1961) 55-56.

[7]Joseph Campbell, *The Power of Myth* with Bill Moyers, ed. Betty Sue Flowers (New York: Doubleday, 1988) 22.

[8]Barbara C. Sproul, *Primal Myths, Creating the World* (San Francisco: Harper & Row, 1979) 11.

[9]Jacques Waardenburg, "Symbolic Aspects of Myth," *Myth, Symbol, and Reality*, ed. Alan M. Olson, vol. 1 of the Boston University Studies in Philosophy and Religion, ed. Leroy S. Rouner (Notre Dame, Indiana: University of Notre Dame Press, 1980) 64.

[10]Alan W. Watts, "Foreword," Charles H. Long, *Alpha: The Myths of Creation* (Toronto: Collier Books, 1969) xi.

[11]Campbell 55.

[12]John Pemberton, "Eshu-Elegba: The Yoruba Trickster God," *African Arts* October 1976: 66.

[13]Philip Freund, *Myths of Creation* (Levittown, New Jersey: Transatlantic Arts, 1975) 233.

[14]Gregory Bateson, *Steps to an Ecology of Mind*; quoted in Bob Samples, *The Metaphoric Mind: A Celebration of Creative Consciousness* (Reading, Massachusetts: Addison-Wesley Publishing Co., Inc., 1976) ix.

[15]Ladislas Segy, *Masks of Black Africa* (New York: Dover Publications, 1976) 8.

[16]Sproul 16.

[17]Kees W. Bolle, *The Freedom of Man in Myth* (Nashville: Vanderbilt UP, 1968) 5.

[18]William G. Doty, *Mythography: The Study of Myths and Rituals* (University: The University of Alabama Press, 1986) 4.

[19]Dorothy Jean Ray, *Eskimo Masks: Art and Ceremony* (Seattle: University of Washington Press, 1975) 10.

[20]Eliade 13.

[21]Mircea Eliade, "The Sacred and the Modern Artist," *Symbolism, the Sacred, and the Arts*, ed. Diane Apostolos-Cappadona (New York: Crossroad, 1988) 83.

[22]Joseph Campbell, *The Inner Reaches of Outer Space: Metaphor as Myth and as Religion* (New York: Alfred van der Marck Editions, 1986) 19.

[23]Marie-Louise von Franz, *Patterns of Creativity Mirrored in Creation Myths* (Zürich: Spring Publications, 1978) 11.

[24]Waardenburg 54.

[25]Ernst Cassirer, *Language and Myth*, trans. Suzanne K. Langer (New York: Dover Publications, 1946) 98.

[26]Elizabeth Abel, "Redefining the Sister Arts: Baudelaire's Response to the Art of Delacroix," *The Language of Images*, ed. W. J. T. Mitchell (Chicago: University of Chicago Press, 1980) 41.

[27]metonymic: using the name of one thing for that of another of which it is an attribute or with which it is associated.

[28]Ernest B. Gilman, "Word and Image in Quarles' *Emblemes*," *The Language of Images*, ed. W. J. T. Mitchell (Chicago: University of Chicago Press, 1980) 63.

[29]Joseph Campbell, *Myths to Live By* (New York: The Viking Press, 1972) 31; specific illustrations of various metaphoric images and an explicit discussion of the ability of metaphor to transcend the mundane and profane by creatively expressing insights into the basic phenomena of life will be developed in the body of this paper; see outline on pages i-ii.

[30]Ian G. Barbour, *Myths, Models and Paradigms: A Comparative Study in Science and Religion* (New York: Harper & Row, 1976) 13.

[31]Segy 10.

[32]Waardenburg 43-44.

[33]Eliade, *Images* 178.

[34]Martin Foss, *Symbol and Metaphor in Human Experience* (Lincoln: University of Nebraska Press, 1949) 146.

[35]Mircea Eliade, "The Symbolism of Shadows in Archaic Religions," *Symbolism, the Sacred, and the Arts*, ed. Diane Apostolos-Cappadona (New York: Crossroad, 1988) 13.

[36]Foss 111; see also *Máscaras Mexicana*: de la Colleción del Ing. Victor José Moya (Mexico: Dirección de Museo de Instituto Nacional de Anthropología e Historia, 1974) 15: "en muchas ocasiones la elaboracion de la mascara es parte del ritual y requiere que el individual este en un estado de pureza fisica y espiritual."

[37]Foss 120.

[38]Eliade, *Images* 173.

[39]David Attenborough, *The Tribal Eye* (London: British Broadcasting Corporation, 1976) 140.

[40]Paul Veyne, *Did the Greeks Believe in their Myths?*

An Essay on the Constitutive Imagination, trans. Paula Wissing (Chicago: The University of Chicago Press, 1988) 110.

[41]Doty 117.

[42]Eliade, *Images* 12.

[43]Foss 110.

[44]Bolle xiii.

[45]Wingert 72.

[46]W. J. T. Mitchell, "Spatial Form in Literature: Toward a General Theory," *The Language of Images*, ed. W. J. T. Mitchell (Chicago: University of Chicago Press, 1980) 298-299.

[47]Campbell, *Inner* 18.

Bibliography

Abel, Elizabeth. "Redefining the Sister Arts: Baude-
laire's Response to the Art of Delacroix." *The
Language of Images*. Ed. W. J. T. Mitchell. Chicago:
University of Chicago Press, 1980. 37-58.

Attenborough, David. *The Tribal Eye*. London: British
Broadcasting Corporation, 1976.

Barbour, Ian G. *Myths, Models and Paradigms: A Comparative Study in Science and Religion*. New York:
Harper & Row, 1976.

Bolle, Kees W. *The Freedom of Man in Myth*.
Nashville: Vanderbilt University Press, 1968.

Campbell, Joseph. *The Inner Reaches of Outer Space:
Metaphor as Myth and as Religion*. New York:
Alfred van der Marck Editions, 1986.

—. *Myths to Live By*. New York: The Viking Press,
1972.

—. *The Power of Myth* with Bill Moyers. Ed. Betty Sue
Flowers. New York: Doubleday, 1988. Print.

Cassirer, Ernst. *Language and Myth*. Trans. Susanne K.
Langer. New York: Dover Publications, 1946.

Doty, William G. *Mythography: The Study of Myths and
Rituals*. University: University of Alabama Press,
1986.

Eliade, Mircea. *Images and Symbols*. Trans. Philip
Mairet. Kansas City: Sheed Andrews and McMeel,
1961.

—. "The Sacred and the Modern Artist." *Symbolism, the
Sacred, and the Arts*. Ed. Diane Apostolos-Cappadona. New York: Crossroad, 1988. 81-85.

—. "The Symbolism of Shadows in Archaic Religions."
Symbolism, the Sacred, and the Arts. Ed.
Diane Apostolos-Cappadona. New York: Crossroad,
1988. 3-16.

Foss, Martin. *Symbol and Metaphor in Human Experience*. Lincoln: University of Nebraska Press, 1949.

Freund, Philip. *Myths of Creation*. Levittown, New
Jersey: Transatlantic Arts, 1975.

Genesis. The Bible. Revised Standard Version.

Gilman, Ernest B. "Word and Image in Quarles' *Emblemes*." *The Language of Images*. Ed. W. J. T. Mitchell. Chicago: The University of Chicago Press, 1980. 59-84.

Gingerich, Willard. "Heidegger and the Aztecs: The Poetics of Knowing in Pre-Hispanic Nahuatl Poetry." *Recovering the Word: Essays on Native American Literature*. Ed. Brian Swann and Arnold Krupat. Berkeley: University of California Press, 1987. 85-112.

Highwater, Jamake. *The Primal Mind: Vision and Reality in Indian America*. New York: Harper & Row, 1981.

Máscaras Mexicanas: de la Colleción del Ing. Victor Jose Moya. Mexico: Dirección de Museos del Instituto Nacional de Antropología e Historia, 1974.

Mitchell, W. J. T. "Spatial Form in Literature: Toward a General Theory." *The Language of Images*. Ed. W. J. T. Mitchell. Chicago: The University of Chicago Press, 1980. 271-299.

Pemberton, John. "Eshu-Elegba: The Yoruba Trickster God." *African Arts* October 1975: 20-27, 66-70, 90-92.

Ray, Dorothy Jean. *Eskimo Masks: Art and Ceremony*. Seattle: University of Washington Press, 1975.

Samples, Bob. *The Metaphoric Mind: A Celebration of Creative Consciousness*. Reading, Massachusetts: Addison-Wesley Publishing Company, Inc., 1976.

Segy, Ladislas. *Masks of Black Africa*. New York: Dover Publications, 1976.

Sproul, Barbara C. *Primal Myths*: *Creating the World*. San Francisco: Harper & Row, 1979.

Taylor, Joshua C. "Two Visual Excursions." *The Language of Images*. Ed. W. J. T. Mitchell. Chicago: The University of Chicago Press, 1980. 25-36.

Veyne, Paul. *Did the Greeks Believe in their Myths? An Essay on the Constitutive Imagination.* Trans. Paula Wissing. Chicago: The University of Chicago Press, 1988.

von Franz, Marie-Louise. *Patterns of Creativity Mirrored in Creation Myths.* Zürich: Spring Publications, 1978.

Waardenburg, Jacques. "Symbolic Aspects of Myth." *Myth, Symbol, and Reality.* Ed. Alan M. Olson. Vol. 1 of The Boston University Studies in Philosophy and Religion. Ed. Leroy S. Rouner. Notre Dame, Indiana: University of Notre Dame Press, 1980. 41-68.

Watts, Alan. "Foreword." Charles H. Long. *Alpha: The Myths of Creation.* Toronto: Collier Book 1969. xi-xii.

Wingert, Paul S. *Primitive Art: Its Traditions and Styles.* New York: New American Library, 1962.

APPENDIX C:
LIBRARY CLASSIFICATION SYSTEMS

The "call numbers" on the card in the card catalog and on the backs of books usually follow the Library of Congress system or the Dewey decimal system. The former is more often used by college libraries and large collections.

THE LIBRARY OF CONGRESS CLASSIFICATION SYSTEM

The Library of Congress system divides all branches of knowledge into twenty-one main groups which are designated by letters of the alphabet.

Then each branch is further divided by the addition of letters and Arabic numerals, permitting endless combinations. The twenty-one groups are:

A	General Works—Polygraphy
B	Philosophy—Religion
C	History—Auxiliary Sciences
D	History—Topography (except America)
E–F	American History and Topography
G	Geography—Anthropology
H	Social Sciences
J	Political Science
K	Law
L	Education
M	Music
N	Fine Arts
P	Language and Literature
Q	Science
R	Medicine
S	Agriculture—Plant and Animal Husbandry
T	Technology
U	Military Science
V	Naval Science
Z	Bibliography and Library Science

To illustrate the subdivision of an area of knowledge, *P* designates the Language and Literature category which subdivides:

P   Philology and Linguistics: General
PA   Greek and Latin Philology and Literature
PB   Celtic Language and Literature
PC   Romance Languages (French, Spanish, Italian)
PD   Germanic Languages

THE DEWEY DECIMAL SYSTEM

All branches of knowledge are divided into ten numbered parts according to hundreds, which are then further divided into specific areas of knowledge. The number on the first line is the call number; below it are other lines indicating the code used for author, a particular work, the edition, the number of copies on hand, and so on. The numbers below indicate ways the number on the first line may appear.

000   General Works
100   Philosophy
200   Religion
300   Social Sciences
400   Language (Philology)
500   Pure Science
600   Useful Arts
700   Fine Arts
800   Literature
900   History

These parts are further divided; the second number in the 800's indicates the country or language of the literature.

810   American Literature in English
820   English and Old English
830   Germanic Literature
840   French, Provençal, Catalan
850   Italian, Rumanian
860   Spanish, Portuguese

APPENDIX D:
REFERENCE MATERIALS AND STYLE MANUALS

Most research will start in the reference room of your library; there you will find many volumes written not to be read but to be used as guides to general and to specialized articles and books about all fields of knowledge. These indexes and general reference books are guides only; they do not contain material you will read; they will not be a part of your bibliography. Quite literally, they are tools that you must learn to use, and no amount of explanation will replace experience and an active imagination. Hence the following list contains only the names of a few reference guides and is not annotated. (See also "Where to Find a Preliminary Bibliography," pp. 18 to 23.)

GENERAL WORKS

There are numerous atlases, dictionaries, and encyclopedias that are too familiar to the average student to need listing here.

GUIDES TO REFERENCE SOURCES

Ackerman, Ernest, and Karen Hartman. *The Information Searcher's Guide to Searching + Researching on the Internet + W*^{3}. Wilsonville: Franklin, Beedle & Associates, 2001.

Armstrong, C. J., and J. A. Large. *Manual of Online Search Strategies*. Boston: Ashgate, 2000.

Balay, Robert, and others, eds. *Guide to Reference Books*, 11th ed. Chicago: American Library Association, 1996.

Bell, Suzanne S. *Librarian's Guide to Online Searching*, 2nd ed. Santa Barbara: Libraries Unlimited, 2009.

Diaz, Karen R. *Reference Sources on the Internet: Off the Shelf and Onto the Web*. New York: Haworth Press, 1997.

Faerber, Marc, ed. *Gale Directory of Databases*. Detroit: Gale Research, 1999.

Hacker, Diana, and Barbara Fister. *Research and Documentation in the Electronic Age*, 3rd ed. Boston: Bedford/St. Martin's, 2002.

Hillard, James M. *Where to Find What: A Handbook to Reference Service*. 4th ed. Metuchen: Scarecrow Press, 2000.

Mann, Thomas, *Oxford Guide to Library Research*, 3rd ed. New York: Oxford University Press, 2005.

Sears, Jean L., and Marilyn K. Moody, *Using Governmental Information Sources: Electronic and Print*, 3rd ed. Phoenix: Oryx Press, 2001.

NOTE: These guides give more detailed information about possible sources than you will find in some indexes (such as those that follow).

BIBLIOGRAPHIES AND SUPPLEMENTS TO THE ONLINE CATALOG

Bibliographic Index: A Cumulative Bibliography of Bibliographies. New York: H. W. Wilson, 1934 to date. (Available online at *http://www.hwwilson.com/databases/biblio.cfm*)

The Cumulative Book Index. New York: H. W. Wilson, 1928–1999. (For books in print in English prior to 1928, see The United States Catalog, 4th ed. New York: H. W. Wilson, 1928).

Essay and General Literature Index. New York: H. W. Wilson, 1934 to date. (Available online at *http://www.hwwilson.com/data bases/eglit.cfm*)

Monthly Catalog of United States Government Publications. Washington, D.C.: Government Printing Office, 1895 to date. (Available online at *http://catalog.gpo.gov*)

BIOGRAPHICAL REFERENCE BOOKS AND DICTIONARIES

Biography Index. New York: H. W. Wilson, 1946 to date. (Available online at *http://www.hwwilson.com/databases/bioind.cfm*)

Current Biography. New York: H. W. Wilson, 1940 to date. (Available online at *http://www.hwwilson.com/databases/cbil-lus.cfm#present*)

Dictionary of American Biography. 22 vols., index, and supplements. New York: Scribner, 1928–1980.

Ethredge, James M., and Barbara Kopala, eds. *Contemporary Authors.* 84 vols. Detroit: Gale Research Corp., 1962 to date.

Parry, Melanie, ed. *Chambers Biographical Dictionary*, 7th. ed. New York: Cambridge University Press, 2002.

Merriam-Webster's Biographical Dictionary, rev. ed. Springfield, Massachusetts: G. & C. Merriam, 1995.

Who's Who. New York: Macmillan, 1849 to date.

REFERENCE BOOKS AND INDEXES ON VARIOUS SUBJECTS

It is almost impossible to draw absolute lines dividing ideas and subjects, to say that one idea concerns just one and no other area of thinking; it is also impossible to define exactly the line distinguishing the subject matter in all the books in a library. The following list therefore makes arbitrary divisions for the sake of convenience. Because reference books are usually kept in the reference room and do not circulate, they are relatively easy to locate without any more information than we have included here.

FINE ARTS AND HUMANITIES

GENERAL:
Humanities Index (http://www.hwwilson.com/ Databases/humani.cfm#Index0)

ART:
Art Index (http://www.hwwilson.com/databases/ artindex.cfm#Index0)
Encyclopedia of American Art
Encyclopedia of World Art
Fine Art Index
Fine Arts: a Bibliographic Guide to Basic Reference Works, Histories, and Handbooks
Index to Art Periodicals
McGraw-Hill Dictionary of Art
The Oxford Dictionary of Art

FILM AND DRAMA:
American Theatre History: An Annotated Bibliography
The Cambridge Guide to World Theatre
Film Literature Index (http://webapp1.dlib. indiana.edu/fli/index.jsp)
A Guide to Critical Reviews
Index to Plays in Collections
International Dictionary of Theatre
International Encyclopedia of Film
McGraw-Hill Encyclopedia of World Drama
Oxford Companion to Film

HISTORY:
Encyclopedia of American History
An Encyclopedia of World History
Historical Abstracts
New Cambridge Modern History

LANGUAGE AND LITERATURE:	*The Cambridge Encyclopedia of Language*
	The Cambridge Guide to Literature in English
	An Encyclopedia of Language
	Funk and Wagnall's Standard Dictionary of Folklore, Mythology, and Legend
	International Encyclopedia of Linguistics
	Literary Research Guide
	M.L.A. International Bibliography
	The Oxford Companion to American Literature
	The Oxford Companion to Classical Literature
	The Oxford Companion to English Literature

MUSIC:	*General Bibliography for Music Research*
	The New Grove Dictionary of American Music
	The New Grove Dictionary of Music
	The New Grove Dictionary of Opera
	The New Oxford Companion to Music

PHILOSOPHY:	*Encyclopedia of Ethics*
	The Encyclopedia of Philosophy
	The Oxford Dictionary of Philosophy
	The Philosophers's Index

THE NATURAL SCIENCES

GENERAL:	*Applied Science and Technology Index (http://www.hwwilson.com/databases/applieds.cfm#Index)*
	General Science Index (http://www.hwwilson.com/Databases/gensci.cfm)
	McGraw-Hill Encyclopedia of Science and Technology (http://www.accessscience.com)
	Van Nostrand's Scientific Encyclopedia

ASTRONOMY:	*The Astronomy Encyclopedia*
	Cambridge Encyclopedia of Astronomy
	Encyclopedia of Astronomy and Astrophysics

BIOLOGY:	*Biological Abstracts*
	Biological and Agricultural Index (http://www.hwwilson.com/databases/bioag.cfm)
	Encyclopedia of Human Biology
	Encyclopedia of Molecular Biology

CHEMISTRY:	*Chemical Abstracts*
	CRC Handbook of Chemistry and Physics
	Handbook of Chemistry and Physics

ENVIRONMENTAL SCIENCES:	*Ecology Abstracts* *Encyclopedia of Ecology and Environmental Management* *Environment Abstracts* *Environment Index* *Pollution Abstracts*

GEOGRAPHY:
Geographical Abstracts
Modern Geography: An Encyclopedic Survey
The World Geographic Encyclopedia

GEOLOGY:
Bibliography and Index of Geology
The Encyclopedia of Field and General Geology
The Oxford Companian to the Earth V

MATHEMATICS AND PHYSICS:
CRC Concise Encyclopedia of Mathematics
Encyclopedia of Physics
Encyclopedic Dictionary of Mathematics
Information Sources in Physics
Physics Abstracts

THE SOCIAL SCIENCES

GENERAL:
International Encyclopedia of the Social Sciences
Social Sciences Index (http://www.hwwilson. com/Databases/socsci.cfm)
The Social Sciences: A Cross-Disciplinary Guide to Selected Resources

ANTHROPOLOGY:
Abstracts in Anthropology
Encyclopedia of Social and Cultural Anthropology

ECONOMICS AND BUSINESS:
Business Periodicals Index (http://www.hwwil son.com/databases/business.cfm#Business)
Encyclopedia of Business Information Sources
McGraw-Hill Encyclopedia of Economics

POLITICAL SCIENCE:
Information Sources in Political Science
International Political Science Abstracts

PSYCHOLOGY:
Dictionary of Philosophy and Psychology
Encyclopedia of Psychology
Library Use: A Handbook for Psychology
Psychological Abstracts

RELIGION: *Encyclopedia of Religion*
The International Standard Bible Encyclopedia
Religion Index

SOCIOLOGY: *Encyclopedia of Sociology*
Sociological Abstracts

TECHNOLOGY

COMPUTER
SCIENCE: *ACM Guide to Computing Literature*
(http://portal.acm.org/dl.cfm)
Computer Abstracts
Computer Science Index
Encyclopedia of Computer Science and
Technology

ENGINEERING: *Engineering Index*
McGraw-Hill Encyclopedia of Engineering

MEDICINE AND *The American Medical Association Encyclopedia*
NURSING: *of Medicine*
Cumulative Index to Nursing and Allied Health
Literature

STYLE MANUALS

Every discipline has its preferred style for the preparation and documentation of scholarly writing. Although most instructors would suggest that you use the formats outlined for you in this book, if you are doing advanced research, you might want to consult the guide used in your field of study, for example:

BUSINESS AND ECONOMICS

Diamond, Harriet, and others. *Executive Writing: A Style Manual for the Business World.* New York: Prentice Hall, 1997.

CHEMISTRY

Coghill, Anne M., and Lorrin R. Garson. *The ACS Style Guide: Effective Communication of Scientific Information.* 3rd ed. Washington, D.C.: American Chemical Society, 2006.

COMMUNICATIONS

Bourhis, John, and others, eds. *A Style Manual for Communication Majors*. New York: McGraw-Hill, 2002.
Updated Printing with 2002 APA Guidelines.

GEOPHYSICAL SCIENCES

Bates, Robert L., ed. *Geowriting: A Guide to Writing, Editing, and Printing in Earth Science*. 5th ed. Alexandria, Virginia: American Geological Institute, 1995.

United States Geological Survey. *Suggestions to Authors of the Reports of the United States Geological Survey*. 7th ed. Washington, D.C.: Government Printing Office, 1991.

GOVERNMENT AND POLITICAL SCIENCE

Lane, Michael K. *Style Manual for Political Science*. American Political Science Association, 2001.

The Bluebook: A Uniform System of Citation, 18th ed. Cambridge, Massachusetts: Harvard Law Review Association, 2005.

HUMANITIES

Gibaldi, Joseph. *MLA Handbook for Writers of Research Papers*. 7th ed. New York: The Modern Language Association of America, 2009.

LINGUISTICS

Linguistic Society of America. Appears in each December issue of the *LSA Bulletin*.

MATHEMATICS

American Mathematical Society. *AMS Author Handbook*. Rev. Providence: American Mathematical Society, 2010.
(Available online at *ftp://ftp.ams.org/pub/author-info/documentation/handbk.pdf*)

MEDICINE

Iverson, Cheryl, and others, eds. *American Medical Association Manual of Style: A Guide for Authors and Editors*. 10th ed. New York: Oxford University Press, 2007.

MUSIC

Radice, Mark A., ed. *Irvine's Writing about Music: A Style Book for Reports and Theses.* 3rd ed. Seattle: University of Washington Press, 1999.

NATURAL SCIENCES

Style Manual Committee. *Scientific Style and Format: The CSE Manual for Authors, Editors, and Publishers.* 7th ed. Wheat Ridge: Council of Science Editors, 2010.

PHYSICS

Publication Board, American Institute of Physics, *Style Manual for Guidance in the Preparation of Papers.* 4th ed. New York: American Institute of Physics, 1990. (Available online at *http://www.aip.org/pubservs/style/4thed/toc.html*)

PSYCHOLOGY

(widely used in the other social sciences)

American Psychological Association. *Publication Manual of the American Psychological Association.* 6th ed. Washington, D.C.: American Psychological Association, 2010.

GENERAL

The following guides are used in a wide variety of fields. (The *MLA Handbook for Writers of Research Papers,* the *Publication Manual of the American Psychological Association,* and *Scientific Style and Format: The CSE Manual for Authors, Editors, and Publishers* previously listed might also be considered general guides because of their wide acceptance outside their own disciplines.)

The Chicago Manual of Style, 16th ed. Chicago: The University of Chicago Press, 2010.

Turabian, below, is a shorter version of this tome.

Rubens, Philip, ed. *Science and Technical Writing: A Manual of Style.* 2nd ed. New York: Routledge, 2000.

Turabian, Kate L. *A Manual for Writers of Term Papers, Theses, and Dissertations.* 7th ed. Chicago: The University of Chicago Press, 2007.

Walker, Janice R. and Todd Taylor. *The Columbia Guide to Online Style.* 2nd ed. New York: Columbia University Press, 2006.

APPENDIX E:
ABBREVIATIONS USED IN RESEARCH

anon.	anonymous
bk., bks.	book(s)
c., ca.	*circa*: "about"; for approximate dates (c. 1884, ca. 1884)
cf.	*confer*: "compare"; not a synonym for *see*
chap., ch., chs.	chapter(s)
col., cols.	column(s)
comp.	compiler, compiled, compiled by
ed., eds.	editor(s), edition(s), or edited by
e.g.	*exempli gratia*: "for example"
et al.	*et alii*: "and others"
et seq.	*et sequens*: "and the following" (or ff., which is shorter)
ex.	example
f., ff.	and the following page(s) (pp. 79f. or pp.79ff)
fig., figs.	figure(s)
ibid.	*ibidem*: "in the same place as quoted above"; refers to title in footnote immediately above; author's name not given; page given if different from the one preceding
i.e.	*id est*: "that is"; preceded by a comma and followed by a comma and list or explanation
ill., illus.	illustration; illustrated by
l., ll.	line(s)
loc. cit.	*loco citato*: "in the place cited"; refers to work fully identified in any previous footnote except the one immediately preceding; preceded by author's last name; never followed by a page number because *loc. cit.* means "in the same location" (page) as in last footnote referring to that source
MS (MSS)	manuscript(s); always capitalized; no period
N.B.	*nota bene*: "take notice; mark well"; always capitalized
n.d.	no date given
no., nos.	number(s)
n.p.	no place of publication (and/or no publisher) given
op. cit.	*opere citato*: "in the work cited"; preceded by author's last name and followed by page number

	(because *op. cit.* stands for title only); refers to work cited previously but not immediately above
p., pp.	page(s)
passim	"throughout the work, here and there"; (p. 37 et passim means p. 37 and other scattered pages; or pp. 37–42 passim)
pl., pls.	plate(s)
pseud.	pseudonym, pen name (Lewis Carroll, Mark Twain)
pt.	part
q.v.	*quod vide*: "which see"
rev.	reviewed by; revised or revised by; revision
rpt.	reprint
sc.	scene
sec. secs.	section(s)
sic	"thus"; not an abbreviation; used within brackets to indicate that an error in quote is in the original: "It was to [*sic*] bad."
st.	stanza
tr., trans.	translator, translation, translated by
v., vv.	verse(s)
viz.	*videlicet*: "namely"; use with or without a period; usage varies
vol., vols.	volume(s); capitalize only before Roman numeral: Vol. VII; 9 vols.

APPENDIX F:
ROMAN NUMERALS

I	**V**	**X**	**L**	**C**	**D**	**M**
1	5	10	50	100	500	1000

To read a number with two or more Roman numerals, start with the larger numeral and subtract what is to the left; add what is to the right.

If a numeral is between two of greater value, subtract it from the second and then add that number (the remainder) to the first:

$$MCMLXXI = 1971$$

A bar over a numeral multiplies it by 1000. Roman numerals may be written in capitals or in lower case.

IX = 9　　　XXXII = 32　　　XL = 40　　　CL = 150
CD = 400　　CDV = 405
DC = 600　　CM = 900　　$\overline{IV}$ = 4000

Use Roman numerals in capitals (IV, XII, CDL) when you want:

to indicate volumes of books in series;
to number the acts in a play;
to number the books (or the cantos) of a long poem;
to identify different people with the same name (George III);
to indicate major divisions in an outline.

Use Roman numerals in lowercase (ii, iv, xii) when you want

to number all prefatory pages including outline and table of contents;
to identify scenes in a drama.

APPENDIX G:
BASIC PUNCTUATION

Punctuating your research paper will be easy if you learn these basic rules that apply to the structures or patterns most frequently used in writing. If you keep the following rules in mind, especially those pertaining to the use of the comma, your paper will be clear and effective.

1. The Apostrophe

a. Use an apostrophe with an *s* to show possession (belonging to): Mary's hat, the heart's desire. *Except*, if the word ends in *s*, then add the apostrophe after the *s*: the Smiths' book (belonging to the Smith family). On occasion, for the sake of pronunciation, a word ending in *s* forms the possessive by adding *es*: The Williamses book (belonging to the Williams family).

b. Use an apostrophe to show that a letter has been omitted: it's/it is; who's/who is; there's/there is.

NOTE: Possessive pronouns have their own forms and do not require an apostrophe: mine, yours, his, their(s), its.

2. The Comma

Do not use a comma unless one of the following rules apply:

a. Use a comma before a coordinating conjunction (or, and, but, for, yet, nor, etc.) in a compound sentence: I did my work, but I forgot to hand it in.

b. Use a comma between items (nouns, clauses, phrases, etc.) in a series of three or more, except before the last item when a conjunction is used: I bought apples, oranges, peaches, and bananas.

c. Use a comma between adjectives preceding a noun: This is a quiet, peaceful hotel. *Except*, if you cannot substitute *and* for the comma, do not use the comma: I have a small black cat.

d. Use a comma after an introductory modifier: Yes, I did it. Well, I'm going now.

e. Use a comma after an introductory prepositional phrase *only* if the phrase is long: In order to succeed in college and prepare for the future, one must study.

163

f. Use a comma to prevent misreading: Once inside, the dog began to bark.

g. Use commas to set off an appositive (an expression following a noun which means the same thing and can be used in place of the noun): Larry Jones, the student standing by the door, scored highest on the exam.

h. Use commas to set off a parenthetical statement (an expression inserted to explain or emphasize): Mary, for example, never studied. John, on the other hand, always did.

i. Use commas to set off a direct address: His comments, my dear friend, cannot be repeated.

j. Use commas to set off an expression inserted into a direct quotation: "Now," he said, "the class is dismissed."

k. Use a comma to show contrast: This is a college, not a university. She is a freshman, not a senior.

l. Use commas to set off a nonrestrictive clause or phrase (an expression that is not necessary for understanding, but does provide additional information): My mother, who is a teacher, came to see me.

m. Use commas to set off an absolute phrase (an expression consisting of a noun or pronoun and a participle that modifies the sentence as a whole): Weather permitting, we can study together tonight.

n. Use a comma before *such as* when it is used to introduce an example: She is interested in many occult subjects, such as magic, astrology, and mind reading.

3. The Semicolon

a. Use a semicolon to separate two independent clauses not joined by a conjunction: I went to see him; he was not there.

b. Use a semicolon between equal elements that contain commas: John, president; Paula, vice-president; Jane, treasurer; and so on.

4. The Colon

Use a colon after a complete statement to draw attention to what follows: She had many hobbies: painting, swimming, tennis, and reading.

5. Quotation Marks

a. Use quotation marks before and after words that are exactly copied: "Well," Mary said, "this is a happy day." Note the position of the quotation marks *after* the comma and the period.

b. Use quotation marks to identify titles of essays, individual poems, songs, stories, which are part of larger works.

6. The Hyphen

Use a hyphen between words used as a single modifier before a noun: He is a well-known writer. This is a half-finished job.

7. Underlining

Underline titles of books, magazines, and other complete works.

In addition to these basic rules, see the index for particular marks of punctuation discussed in various sections of this book.

INDEX

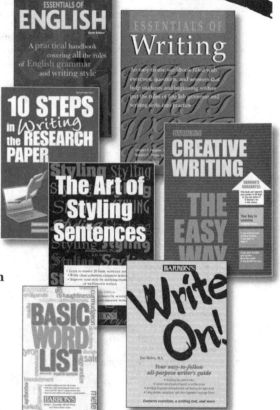